Signs from GOD

When there is no other explanation

. . . it just has to be!

Sharon Shabinaw
Arlene Garrett

What supporters and followers have to say about the stories being shared on the Sykesville Online Community page about this mother and daughter's journey together:

✝ *"This has been my MOST FAVORITE topic on SOC EVER!!! Thank you & God bless you for opening this up for discussion. It far outweighs any negative posts in the past."*

✝ *"I absolutely LOVE hearing these kinds of stories, they are so uplifting. Good luck with your book!"*

✝ *"It is nice to know others believe in the joys, warmth, and emotional ties we can have with our loved ones that have passed on."*

✝ *"This is a great project and reminds us of our faith. You can 'hear' the enthusiasm in everyone's story which I think represents how meaningful it was to them."*

✝ *"I think your post was a bright spot for a lot of people today missing loved ones."*

✝ *"Thank you for starting such an amazing thread. It is just what I needed today!"*

✝ *"What a wonderful post you created today. So many people in our community sharing their faith in our Lord, bringing people together. Well done."*

✝ *"I would be honored if you used my story. Who knows, maybe it will help someone else."*

This book is dedicated to:

✠ *Our Lord and Savior, Jesus Christ, who has led us on this journey and directed the path we were to take throughout this process to get our book published. It is for Him this book was written in hopes of sharing the many different ways He communicates with all of us.*

✠ *Our wonderful family: Sharon's husband, Tom, who is the love of her life and has graciously supported and encouraged both of us every step of the way; our children, grandchildren, and Arlene's great grandchildren . . . You are our World!*

✠ *Our best friends of many years, Karen, Gloria, Sue, Jean, Carol, and Linda who have been by our side and seen us through all of the good times, bad times and in between times.*

✠ *A special thank you to the community of Sykesville, Maryland, for their willingness to share such personal stories and their excitement for having them published.*

✠ *A special dedication to all of our loved ones who have passed before us to be with our Lord and Savior. They are all truly missed!*

✠ *And to all of those who have truly supported us over the years. You know who you are and we are forever grateful!*

Acknowledgements

It is with the utmost respect and gratitude that we acknowledge the following individuals for their love, *support, time, talents, resources, ideas, and feedback.* For without them, this book would not be possible.

Kelly Norman (Daughter; Book Cover Designer, and Social Media Supporter)

Cindy C Bennett (Author, Editor, Formatter, and Mentor)

Tristi Pinkston (Author; and another great source of recommendations along the way!)

Table of Contents

Preface

From the moment God spoke to me in a small, soft voice, prompting me to document the signs I have received from Him, it's as if He has been speaking directly to me. Throughout this entire journey, I have continually received signs from Him leading me every step of the way. From the initial conception, to prompting my community to share their stories, all the way to the book cover, it was God who made the decisions. I've only been following His lead. One night I prayed for His help on the front cover picture, and at that exact moment, in the middle of prayer, He answered. While my original idea was completely different, His was the only one that now made sense and it all tied into the *Signs from God*.

Then, during the editing process, there was a twist and yet another sign from God when we recognized the need to share my mother's story and testimony of the miracle she experienced after suffering for five years with a nervous breakdown. Her testimony has been the inspiration and driving force through this entire

1

journey, and our lives. Sharing her testimony, and now co-authoring *Signs from God*, is giving us the opportunity to begin our journey together towards our ultimate goal of sharing her story much sooner. We feel this book is paving the way for us to do just that. You too will recognize my mother's testimony as the backbone for this book and our message of hope knowing God is in control.

As you read how God has touched our lives and others, you will realize that this project has truly been God driven. He continues to lead us, pushing us down His chosen path to the life He has in store for us. Are you seeking signs from God? I believe these stories will bring you comfort and increase your awareness of the signs He is providing and how He is speaking to all of us.

1
God's Presence

God's presence has always been a part of my life. Sometimes it's stronger than others, sometimes I have periods of doubt. When I was an adolescent my mother battled with a nervous breakdown for nearly five years. She was in and out of hospitals and experienced so much pain and torment that I could not help but wonder *why*. Why would God put her through such a traumatic experience? She was a good person, a great mother, a loyal friend that would do anything for anyone . . . I could go on and on, so why her? She firmly believed in God, yet five long years passed before her miraculous healing took place.

My mother's story and testimony of the "miracle" that she so vividly describes, continues to affect our lives every day. The presence of God and His power has pulled my mother and I through many situations in our lives. We are grateful for the blessings He has given us. Even though she struggled for several years in a nearly constant state of flux and despair, He was always there with us. I can now recognize that He didn't put us through anything we couldn't handle. When she could take no more, He healed her. She is stronger now than she has ever been in her life, and we continue to follow His lead by sharing her story and miracle. We know He did not put her through that ordeal in vain. It is our mission to tell her story and spread the word of God in the hope of helping others that may be suffering from anxiety and depression, or are in need of hope. We hope the sharing of her story will encourage others to never give up hope knowing that God is with us always, and He will get us through the trials we must endure in life.

Living through my mother's nervous breakdown has made me strong, as well. I learned many years after my mother's miraculous healing of the actual events and the specific miracle she experienced. As you can imagine, from this experience my understanding of God's power has become a guiding presence in my life. He wants all of us to have faith in Him. He shows us signs all of the time. We only need to learn to recognize those signs, and understand that the thoughts that seem to just appear in our head as intuition are actually God talking to us in His small, soft voice. I have received many of these thoughts and whispers from God lately to share my signs with you, and to capture some signs from others as well, because He speaks to all of us. To some He may speak loudly, to some perhaps He whispers, and to others the message is so profound that it is unmistakable.

Over the years I have had many moments in my life where God has made his presence known. The first sign I remember was in 1990 while going through the decision process of whether or not to end my marriage. I had two small children at the time. The agony of what life would be like for them without a father in their life, and how I would be able to support the three of us if we were on our own, seemed overwhelming to me. It took several years for me to come to terms with my decision and to be financially secure enough to make a move. I know God put the right people in my life, and the right job, that has led me to where I am today. He took the weight from my shoulders and brought me to a place of peace. At the time, it was hard to understand why, but looking back I know that God was very much in control. He has led me on this journey every step of the way.

As I learned and slowly matured spiritually, I have recognized the clear signs indicating that everything happens for a reason. Prior to making my final decision on whether or not to separate from my husband, I was laid-off from a job I loved and had worked for six years. I found a new job, but little did I know that I would also find my future husband there.

After working at that company for two years, we learned that we were both in the same situation. He was in the process of going through a divorce as well, having been married for many years and fathering three daughters. Eventually, we started to communicate about the situation we both found ourselves in.

One day he was very distraught and I suggested he speak with a therapist. He thought we should start dating, but that was the last thing I needed as I was just starting to get my life to a place where I felt I could move out on my own. I knew if something were to happen between the two of us and it didn't work out, I'd be the one who would have to give up my job. He had been there much longer than I and was further up the corporate ladder. As a new single mom on my own, dating a co-worker seemed like a colossally bad idea.

I remember well the night everything changed. It was December 3, 1996. He had an appointment scheduled with his therapist. I decided to meet him afterward, as friends, so we could talk about how it went. When we met he told me he was stood-up by his therapist and had been driving around just waiting to meet with me. We talked for a couple hours, and then he put his arm around me and announced he didn't need therapy as long as he had me in his life. I can't explain it, but the moment he put his arm around me, I just knew he was the man for me and that everything was going to be fine. I felt so protected and safe I knew our relationship was meant to be. It sounds corny and cliché to say I saw fireworks and just knew. I didn't see fireworks, but I definitely felt something—something I have never felt before. From that night on, we were more than just friends. The following weekend, he went with me to find an apartment for me and my boys. Things began to happen pretty quickly for us. I moved out December 31st and he moved into his apartment February 1st. By June he was living with me and the boys, and we began working on blending our families.

During this time, an opening presented itself with the company I was originally laid-off from, which enabled me to return to a different position with an increase in salary and the ability to have a flexible schedule. I seemed to have it all and was right back where I started, with the same company I loved. There was no doubt in my mind it was meant to be, and that everything that had happened did so for a reason.

From that point forward I grew closer to God and my beliefs. I saw God's work in everything. There were multiple signs over the years. Nothing specific—just general things, like being spared in an accident, a job interview that came when I needed it most, or people who were brought into my life for a specific reason or a season. I had the insight to recognize His signs, and believe in His presence. As I began recognizing these more and more, I decided to capture and document the signs that I had been, and would be, given.

When He spoke to me and prompted me to take this a step further, I reached out to other people in hopes of capturing their experiences as well to share with other believers or those struggling to believe. God has our best interests in mind, and He is in control. He already knows the path we will take, and He will guide us, directing our path toward His plan for our lives. While we may falter and take a bad turn, He is always there leading us back toward His chosen path for us.

I can't tell you how many times He has placed obstacles in my path during this writing journey. At times, life just happens to step in the way of your goal or tasks at hand, but always remember there is a reason. These obstacles, mountains, and valleys that we go through are all opportunities where we can learn and grow into stronger individuals. We need to recognize His greatness in all of the challenges He may throw our way, and consider them the blessings they truly are. Every obstacle He sent my way turned into a blessing. At times, it was a much needed break to focus, take care of myself or a loved one in need, or simply time to recognize where He was redirecting my path. Regardless of the obstacle, He always gets me back on track feeling more motivated than ever. It is clear to me that this book is His doing and not mine. When I am struggling with, "How am I going to do this? What is the next step? Who do I reach out to for assistance?" it is He who continually shows me the way. Philippians 4:6 says, *"Do not be anxious about anything, but in every situation, by prayer and petition, with thanksgiving, present your requests to God."* This is so true! I ask, and within moments I am led on a trail of internet clicks until I find just the right link to get the answers I'm looking for. Without fail, it is He who keeps me motivated and on the right track, following His will for me.

2
My Mother's Story

For those of you that may have experienced a miracle or an encounter with God that was so profound it was unmistakable, my mother's story will bring feelings of overwhelming peace and comfort back to the surface in knowing that God is in control. Every time I hear her testimony, chills overcome me and memories flood back to those days and the events that led to her miraculous healing in 1980. The following is an introduction written by my mother, Arlene Garrett and co-author, explaining her thoughts and feelings of suffering with a nervous breakdown.

Life is funny sometimes. It can be a real rollercoaster ride. When you think you have it all together, and you seem to know just what you're doing and where you're going, life has a way of turning everything around. When my daughter Sharon and I started out on our writing journey together a little over a year ago, we were excited to finally put pen to paper and begin our book, *A Mountain to Climb*. At least, that is how we started out. We worked on it for many months. This will be a book from both the mother's perspective, as the patient suffering through a nervous breakdown that will include flashbacks from her daughter's perspective at a vulnerable time in her life when she needed her mother the most. I believe it is proving to be very therapeutic for both of us and we have learned a lot from each other as we compared notes. We are still actively working on this book as well, and hope to have it published by the end of 2016.

In the interim, we kept receiving signs from God and wondered what was happening. We are so very connected to our thoughts and feelings and had many conversations about the way we both felt we were being pulled. Then everything seemed to just fall into place for the writing of this book and the opportunity for me to share my testimony of the miraculous healing that took place in my life in 1980. I truly believe that everything has happened just the way it was supposed to happen by getting this book out first. All the glory goes to God, and the main reason for writing *A Mountain to Climb* is to get the message out there of this miraculous testimony. Thank you, God, for the signs and nudges along the way that have allowed my story to be heard much sooner than I ever dreamed possible. But then, all things are possible through God!

It is hard for me to believe that so many years have passed since the most traumatic time in my life. I never thought back then that I would be here to tell my story and testify of the miraculous healing that I experienced in 1980. Years ago, depression and anxiety wasn't recognized as an illness. People just didn't want to talk about it. This was a hush, hush, taboo subject. People were made to feel that they were different, or their condition was something to be ashamed of. They were considered a "weak" person. This only made the person suffering with this illness feel even worse.

I thank God for making me well and giving me the courage now, after 35 years, to speak openly and honestly about this devastating illness that affects so many people today. Depression, anxiety attacks, and even worse, a complete nervous breakdown are illnesses just like any other medical condition. I am thankful that today it is being recognized with understanding and empathy for the patient going through such a distressing time.

I realize that through all those years after my healing, and the events in my life that followed, everything happened to get me to where I am today. One of the good things about growing older is you do become wiser and learn from your experiences. As I look back on my past and the people who have come into or out of my life, either for a reason or a season, it has all been part of God's plan for me to do His will in His time, not mine. While I didn't understand at the time, I now see all the puzzle pieces of my life simply falling into place. God has been preparing me all these years to do what I believe is His plan and mission for my life, and that is to serve Him and bring others to know Him as well.

I couldn't help but feel like a failure for having that breakdown so many years ago and feeling so guilty inside, but now I am at peace. Praise the Lord, I have learned to put the past behind me and live each day to the fullest. I know all my suffering was not in vain, and I believe that part of God's plan for me is to help others who are suffering with depression and feelings of hopelessness. Never give up hope—you are never alone. God is always with you! One of the first things I discovered when I was finally healed after five long years was "Footprints". I thought I was all alone for so long and wondered, "Why, God, did you leave me?" I truly believe that it was God who led me to read "Footprints" after He healed me. It was then that I understood. What an awe inspiring moment that was for me.

Life is a journey. We will always have trials and tribulations to endure. It is so easy to give up when you are surrounded by darkness and gloom, but never give up the hope that beneath those dark clouds in your life, there is a blue sky and the sun will shine once again. Dance as though no one is watching, love as though you have never loved before, sing as though no one can hear you, and live as though heaven is on Earth. Hope in the Lord, and He will see you through.

In retrospect, as I look back to the days when my depression and anxiety first started, I believe I seemed to be looking too far ahead in time. My thoughts were, *What if this?* or *What if that?* and those kind of thoughts always seemed to be going on in my mind. I would never want to live through those horrific years again, but I have learned a lot about myself and have certainly grown from this experience. I now know to take one day at a time, and that nothing can happen to me today or any day that God and I together can't handle. Life here on Earth is very short in perspective, so we must live it to the fullest every day. God is in control of our lives. We just need to give all of our burdens to Him and let it go. I feel very blessed to have the love and support of my family and friends throughout this journey. I pray for God to direct my path to things undone and continue to guide me for His will to be done.

Since my healing, I have tried to live my life to make God proud of me by helping others whenever I can. I have been an active member of my church, and enjoy singing in the choir and contemporary band. I studied to become a Stephen Minister, as well as a hospice volunteer to bring comfort to those who are in need. I try to live by the golden rule of treating others as I would want them to treat me, but that hasn't always worked out in my favor. But that's okay, because I know God is always with me. I've had to make some major decisions in my marriage and divorce that were extremely hard for me to do. I took my marriage vows very seriously, so it was a real struggle to do what I felt was the right thing. I spent many sleepless nights talking to God and praying for His guidance. Then, one day many years ago, I read the following statement and it made sense to me. It goes like this, "What you program into the jukebox of your life will play through the stereo system of your environment; if you can't dance to the song that's playing, change it!" That saying has stuck with me, and I will keep on dancing for as long as God is willing.

The road has not been easy to where I find myself today, but I am at peace with the decisions I have made for my life with help and guidance through the grace of God.

There was a light at the end of a dark tunnel for me—I just couldn't see it at the time I was going through the fog of my breakdown. I only wish I knew then what I know now when it comes to giving our burdens to God. We don't have to carry these worries, trials, and tribulations that life throws at us alone. When we reach up to God, He will reach down for us to guide and see us through whatever we may be troubled with at that time.

May God Bless you and keep you in His loving care always, and may you find comfort and hope after reading my testimony that miracles can and do happen.

3

Arlene's Testimony

*"For I know the plans I have for you," declares
the Lord, "plans to prosper you and not to harm
you, plans to give you hope and a future."*

NIV Jeremiah 29:11

Do you believe in miracles? I do, and as I share
my story with you, the following testimony of my
experience will explain why. I have had several
spiritual encounters, but the most meaningful, and the
one I want to share with you now, was truly a miracle.
I experienced it, I lived through it, and it changed my
life forever!

After five agonizing years living with a nervous
breakdown, three suicide attempts, shock treatments,
and being given every available antidepressant and
tranquilizer on the market, I was ultimately healed.
However, my healing didn't come from doctors or
drugs, because doctors had given up all hope for me.
As I lay in a state mental hospital bed having heard the
doctors tell my family there was nothing more they

could do and there was no hope for me, my healing came from *above*. I was given the breath of life and *never* would I *ever* be the same again.

It's been 35 years since I was healed, and for all those years I kept my story hidden, stifled in my mind and heart for fear of people not believing me or thinking that I was crazy. Believe me, this is not the case. I know God did not put me through all those years of suffering in vain. I know He has a mission for me to accomplish.

My illness began in 1976. I was thirty two years old at the time and in the process of going through a very painful divorce. It was the most difficult time of my life. The depression and sadness that invaded and took over my mind and body was so overwhelming that I was unable to do the simplest of tasks. The anxiety attacks brought on by my mind racing made me feel like I was dying. During the last four months of my illness, a series of events happened to me that can only be truly understood by someone who has experienced a similar life threatening trauma.

A lot of my suffering and things that happened to me during my breakdown still remain a mystery to this day. I believe much of my behavior was related to the side effects from all the drugs and tranquilizers the doctors had me on. I only know that my mind and body was not mine during those years. I was constantly tormented by lack of sleep and in such pain from involuntary movements I was unable to control. I thought the pain would never end.

From 1976 until 1980 I was in and out of hospitals and was admitted seven different times to Spring Grove Mental Hospital. The doctors kept telling me if I went back to my husband I would not get well and would probably return to the hospital, but in my mind I wanted to be happily married and fought my true feelings. The doctors were right. But the last time I was admitted was to be different for me. Little did I know then that 1980 was to be my worst year and my best year all in one.

During my final admission to the state mental hospital, I was given a weekend leave to spend with my parents when a change started coming over my body. Up until then, my body was not at peace. I can best describe it as a feeling of having a veil inside me covering my heart, soul, mind and spirit. It was a feeling of perhaps being possessed by demons. It was horrific! My body would shake all over and I could barely talk. No one knew what was happening to me, especially not myself.

I was in a room with my father where there were

two twin beds, and between them was a night table where a statue of Jesus stood. I turned the statue around. At that moment, I hated Jesus. When my father came in the room and saw Jesus' back turned, he asked me, "Arlene, did you do that? Did you turn Jesus' back to you?" All I could say

17

was, "I HATE JESUS! I HATE GOD for making me sick!" My Father said, "Don't you ever let me hear you say that again! God is not making you sick!". He turned the statue around and walked out of the room. I had never seen my father so angry at me! But again, I turned the statue around.

As I paced nervously back and forth, suddenly my hands started to come together until they got close and then, like a magnet, they came together in a prayer position. A very powerful force drove me to my knees right at my father's bedside. It was clear that a force greater than you or I was overtaking my body. I knelt there for a long time, unable to move. I knew God had put me in this prayer position. He wanted me to be well, but first God wanted me to come to him in prayer. It wasn't as though I didn't pray before, because I did. Perhaps it was that I didn't truly *believe* that God would make me well. It was hard to really "Let Go and Let God."

Unable to move and still kneeling at my father's bed, I could hear my mother calling me from the other room. "Come out of that bedroom," she said. "What are you doing in there?" I became fearful because I had no control over what was happening to me, and I felt she wouldn't understand. I walked toward the living room where she was reading the paper. I kept praying, *"Please God, don't make me do this, or my mother will be mad."* But again, a powerful force started making my hands come together and when they got inches apart, like a magnet, they were in a prayer position.

For the second time, I was forced down to my knees, only this time, right in the middle of the living room floor in front of where my mother was sitting. Unable to understand that I had no control over my own body, she immediately got up, hollered at me to stop this and then called my sister to take me back to the hospital. I felt doomed. I knew what was happening around me but I couldn't even speak at this point. Totally catatonic, I could not respond to the shouting that was being directed at me. It was as if I was paralyzed. My mind was spinning. My worst fear was if they took me back to the hospital, I'd never leave again. Unfortunately, no one else knew what I was feeling or thinking. To my family I had really gone off the deep end. Consequently, they took me back to the hospital a day early.

It was truly the worst day of my life. Seeing the tears roll down my father's cheeks and in my sister's eyes was absolutely devastating to me. I had hurt them so much by being sick, but I had no power over what was happening to me. When we arrived at the hospital, the doctor put me in a room all alone. My body was shaking and trembling from head to toe. I was never more terrified in my life as I was at that moment. I'd just overheard the doctor tell my father and sister out in the hallway that he was sorry, he didn't think I would ever be well again and there was nothing more that could be done. All hope at that point in time was missing. I lay there listening to the sobs and then the heavy metal door closed. They were gone. I was never more alone than at that moment.

It was then that it happened. I started talking to God, like I am talking to you right now. It was a very short prayer. "Dear God, please make me well or take me home with you. I can't take anymore." As I lay there, paralyzed with fear, calmness began to come over my entire body. It started at my toes and worked its way up until it reached my heart. The shaking and trembling gradually subsided. Not only was I feeling calm, but also peaceful. It was the most beautiful feeling I can ever describe. It was as if the veil was lifting from deep inside that had had control over me for so long. Then, suddenly, I felt a warm puff of air in my mouth adding to this now peaceful, calm body. Tears welled up in my eyes and rolled down my cheeks as I knew instantly I was healed. I was well, and I knew it. I had just experienced a miracle.

For months before this had happened to me, I could not sleep or eat. I literally watched the clock hands go around from one hour to the next. I was never sleepy, always wide awake. This is one of the mysteries I still don't understand. I had lost so much weight that my body was starting to look like a skeletal figure. Once I was healed I began to get hunger pains and, for the first time in a long time, I was able to eat a full meal. That night I fell asleep for about an hour. The next night, I slept for two hours, then three, four, five hours each night and so on until I was able to sleep through the entire night.

In the days that followed, the doctors and staff could hardly believe the transformation that took place when they began to see the "new" me; physically, mentally and spiritually. It was wonderful! I could actually feel the spirit moving from within. Before this miraculous healing took place, I had no interest in reading, or in anything for that matter. Now, I was being led to spiritual booklets that were in the hospital's day room. I would open at random to a page that I was meant to read. When this happened time after time, it was like a light bulb going on in my head. Everything seemed to be coming together for me after all those years of being incapacitated. I knew God was talking to me. I could feel it through my entire body. There was no doubt in my mind that I was truly healed.

When I was released, part of the condition was to go as an "outpatient" for one-on-one therapy and stay on my medication. I told the doctors that medication didn't make me well and I didn't need it anymore. But of course, I was in no position to argue with the doctors and I didn't want to be labeled "crazy," so I had to watch what I said. Deep down though, I had no doubt. The doctors insisted, saying I would have a relapse if I did not continue to take the medication.

For the first few weeks after my discharge from the hospital, I weaned myself off the medication. For six months I went on my weekly visits and saved each prescription that was written until my last visit when I showed the doctor all the prescriptions that I had saved and never taken.

The doctor could not believe his eyes. He was absolutely astonished as he looked at me and said, "Are you telling me you have not been on any medication for the past six months?"

My doctor discharged me and wrote on my chart, "A complete success story!" To this date, I have never been back to the therapist, psychiatrist, or the state mental hospital.

Fast forward to 35 years later, today, I live each day to the fullest, taking one day at a time. There is never a day that goes by that I don't thank God for making me well and giving me back the gift of life. I now know that nothing will happen today or any day that God and I together can't handle.

You may ask me, "Do you feel angry at God for making you suffer all those years?"

My answer is, "No!" I feel blessed because he chose *me* to witness and deliver His message.

I've come to realize that just as God was not the cause of my darkest hour, He also never abandoned me throughout my ordeal.

"Do you believe in miracles?" Yes, oh, yes. I am a walking miracle.

4

Sharon's Signs from God

After reading my mother's testimony, you can only imagine what she went through, and what I, as a young adolescent, went through witnessing my mother experience such torment, not knowing if she was ever going to be the same again. Learning years later of the miracle she experienced, the circumstances that led to her breakdown, and witnessing her transformation into one of the strongest women I have ever known, has made me what I am today. The events of her life have ultimately altered mine. Her spirituality has become my own. As I began to mature, I too was able to recognize signs I was beginning to receive from God. As we begin our journey of telling her story, it is the signs from God that have brought us here that I would like to share with you.

Post-it Note

I don't remember the exact day in the summer of 1990, but I do remember the moment I received my first sign from God.   It's a moment that I believe everyone remembers because it is an awakening inside of you. A feeling of pure love and peace comes over you, total astonishment, a life-altering moment.

My boys were three and four years of age at the time and I was going through a very difficult time in my life. My marriage was not good. My husband at the time was very controlling and sometimes verbally and mentally abusive to me and our boys. To this day they are troubled by events from their early childhood. I wish I could change that for them. At that point in my life I could not afford to be on my own with my children. I'd just recently returned to the workforce after doing in-home daycare for several years. I attempted to leave several times, and once I actually packed everything up and planned to move in with my mother. He insisted, however, that we either come back home or he would move to Kansas and never see the boys again. I still wanted them to have a relationship with their father so I went back.

One day, sitting in my office, feeling depressed, distraught, and simply not able to concentrate on anything, I mindlessly dropped a drop or two of whiteout onto a sticky pad and folded the paper in half. My mind seemed to be everywhere. So many questions I kept asking myself. I remember thinking, *"What should I do? What can I do to make a difference? Would we be better off without him in our lives? Or do I take a leap of faith for the sake of all of us?"*

I opened the piece of paper and saw a cross in the seam where I had dropped the whiteout. I sat there in awe, practically breathless, in total amazement. Was this a sign from God? I knew it had to be, because when I held the piece of paper up to the light I could see the figure of Jesus on that cross when He paid for our sins so that we can live on.

I was immediately overcome with peace knowing that God was in control, and from that point forward I believed that everything happens for a reason. I took one day at a time doing what I needed to do for my children and myself. While this planning took time and many more struggles, I was eventually able to break away and free myself and my boys.

Chris

I had a dream once about my son, Chris, who was around thirteen years old at the time—old enough that I didn't need to check on him in the middle of the night. In this dream his hair caught on fire and I was desperately trying to put it out while screaming the whole time. In my dream, I was able to put out the fire by dunking his head in a bucket of ice water. It was so traumatic and realistic that I woke up and was immediately overcome with panic so great that I had to check on him. When I did, he was burning up with fever. He was fine just the day before. He complained he was cold and had the chills, yet he didn't want to wake me up. God works in mysterious ways, and it just goes to prove that everything happens for a reason. Was it ironic that the fire represented his fever and the ice water his chills? I believe God spoke to me.

I'm Coming for Nana

My grandfather had been with the Lord since December 22, 1988, and not once had I ever dreamt of him. Yes, of course I missed him dearly, but I never had a dream about him. It wasn't until January of 2005 when I had the most vivid dream I have ever had in my life. In this dream my grandfather came to me. I ran up, sat in his lap and hugged him so tight. I could actually feel him and smell his breath. My grandfather had a unique odor to his breath that I remember from a child, and in this dream he was there just as clear as day. I could see, feel, and smell his presence.

I asked him, "How? What are you doing here?"

His reply was simple. "I'm coming to get your grandmother."

'Nana' is what us grandchildren called her, and she was not doing very well. She was at an assisted living home at the time, and really starting to fail. I was very close to my grandmother. She always said I was her favorite, but she probably said that to all of us. When my grandfather passed away, I took it very hard. I know that he recognized that—even from the other side—and he knew how hard I would take losing her. Later I realized he had even more insight.

On May 14, 2005 I was on my way to visit my grandmother with my stepdaughter, who is a nurse, and our firstborn granddaughter who was just born May 3rd. We knew Nana wouldn't be around much longer and we wanted her to see the baby as we knew it would make her happy. We didn't expect her to die before we ever got to see her. When we walked in, the care providers looked bewildered and speechless. They said it wasn't a good time and that we should wait in the living room. I saw Nana hunched over the table and they quickly wheeled her back to her room. We stood in the living room with the baby for a few minutes until I couldn't take it any longer. I informed them that my daughter was a nurse and they welcomed us to the room for assistance. It was my stepdaughter, Kristin, who pronounced my grandmother's time of death. While this was very traumatic for both of us, I remembered that dream I had months ago and a sense of peace came over me knowing that Pop-Pop was there with us, escorting Nana to the gates of Heaven. Had it not been for Pop-Pop coming to me in my dream, I know the outcome of emotions would have been so much greater. I am so thankful for the insight he had in knowing I would be the one there at the time and that he came to prepare me for such a great loss.

The Cross

In the spring of 2010 the economy was not in good shape. My husband had been laid off from work for over a year. He was troubled and depressed. At our age, it wasn't easy finding a job without a college degree or experience. We had gone through most of our savings and he was at a very low point in his life despite my attempts to reinforce my belief that 'everything happens for a reason' and that the right job would come.

One Sunday afternoon he was leaning over the counter while I was working in the kitchen.

I heard him say under his breath, "God, just show me a sign."

I felt sorry for him and the agony he was putting himself through. It was only minutes later that he walked onto the back deck. Looking down at the ground he saw something shiny. He called for me to come take a look. I don't believe he could believe his own eyes. I went out and looked and I saw a gold cross just lying there in the grass (apparently lost during a cookout the kids had the summer before).

I said to him, "Now there's your sign!"

I picked it up and brought it to him. We both had tears in our eyes as we stood and felt the beauty of the moment. That night we slept peacefully knowing that God had a plan and it would come together if we were patient and believed. It wasn't long after that when he received a job offer—the best job he'd had. Within a few short months he received three substantial raises, making him the bread winner of the family again.

Everything Happens for A Reason

In November of 2012 my mother-in-law, Grace, came to visit for Thanksgiving. Three days after her arrival she received a phone call from her doctor stating she had ovarian cancer and needed to be seen immediately. At 82, she lived in Michigan and had just retired from work that spring. She was in shock and at a loss as to what to do. I took control and made her an appointment at Sinai Hospital in Baltimore, MD. The decision was made that she would stay with us indefinitely and eventually we would move her things and close up her house. We thought the move would happen the next summer anyway, but with her diagnosis the decision was made for her. Was it ironic that God brought her to us with such perfect timing? It was God's plan.

When summer arrived we packed up her house. It was a very rough year, and we were grateful to have so many people's support. My job was something else we were very thankful for. Having the flexibility to work remotely was heaven sent. Grace went through chemotherapy, radiation, and several surgeries before her battle was lost. There were many signs during that time that God was moving within us, and for us, throughout her struggle and treatments. It was obvious that He led us where we needed to be in order to get her to the best doctors and the treatment she needed.

What we didn't know was that His timing was not ours.

On January 28, 2014, we learned the cancer was back and was very aggressive. There was not much hope for a cure at that point. She made the decision she would not undergo any additional chemo. A peace came over her when she made the decision and God lifted the weight from her shoulders. She actually had a sparkle in her eyes that was comforting. I wished the rest of the family could have witnessed that for themselves. Over the next couple of hours I recognized a steady decline in her ability to stay alert. She was ready to be with the Lord. She was released from the hospital the next day under Hospice care and passed away three days later in the comfort of her home, with all of her children by her side.

Later that same year, in November, my Aunt Iris started suffering with stomach pains after having undergone shoulder surgery earlier that month. She went for follow up visits with her doctor and even an ultrasound, but nothing showed up. In December, things were getting worse and questions were not answered. In fact, it seemed like the doctor was brushing them aside to concentrate on the shoulder surgery. It got to the point where we knew something was extremely wrong and we took her to the hospital ourselves. It was then that the nightmare truly began. We learned she had a large mass in her abdomen that had "fingered" everywhere. She was diagnosed with advanced stage ovarian cancer. Within a week she was sent home with Hospice care, where she passed three days later to be with our Lord. I was with my mother and my aunt's family through it all. When Grace was diagnosed, she had time to come to terms with her situation and prepare. My aunt did not have the same opportunity, and the family was just going through the motions and desperately grasping for help and direction while making the toughest decisions of their lives.

I believe God led Grace to our home just in time for us to help her through her cancer diagnosis and passing so that she could be with her loved ones during this horrific time. I also believe that this experience gave me the knowledge and foresight to help my family through the diagnosis and passing of my aunt. I knew what to expect and did my best to prepare my family for the reality of what was to come. The hardest part with my aunt's passing was the fact that this came on so quickly without any warning. At times like this, you have to wonder why. Though we know everything happens for a reason, it happens on His timing and His plan, until one day when it's our time and then we'll all understand!

Real Estate

For years we had considered the thought of upgrading our home to something more modern and spacious. Every time we entertained the idea, in the end we realized that we were perfectly content with our home. It was perfect for just the two of us with our children out on their own and we still had two guest rooms. Our house was plenty big enough with four bedrooms, an office, living room, den, etc. The only thing lacking was an upgraded kitchen and a nice master bedroom. We loved our location, which backed up to the Liberty Reservoir and was surrounded by trees. There was plenty of open space, privacy, and room for the dogs to run. Yet when my mother-in-law, Grace, moved in with us we started contemplating the idea again of upgrading our home and looking for something with an in-law apartment where she would have her own space. We wanted her to have room to spread out and have more of her own things around her. As you read earlier, Grace was fighting a battle with cancer. We were very optimistic and her treatments were going well. We hoped that she would be with us for many years. While she was 82 years old, her mother had lived to be almost 100. She was very active; in fact, and had just retired from CVS. Grace had fought and beat breast cancer years ago, as well as skin cancer. We had no doubt she would survive ovarian cancer as well.

We were all very excited at the thought of moving and quickly began the process of getting our home ready and on the market. We had our realtor showing us homes a couple times a week until we found just the right one. We agreed to put a contract on the home contingent on ours selling. Unfortunately, ours didn't sell in time and we lost the contract. A little disappointed, we started the process again until we found another home. This home we agreed was even better than the first one, so we put a contract on it. The same thing happened. With the market not being good at the time, our house still did not sell. There was someone who wanted to rent, but we didn't want to go through that process. Most of the feedback we received was the fact that the kitchen was outdated.

Time passed and so did Grace. We were lost without her and, after fighting the cancer battle for a year while trying to find just the right home for us; we were worn out. In the end, we decided that God knew all along that Grace was not going to be with us long and we were meant to stay right where we were. Today, we are so glad that house didn't sell because we would have been stuck in a large home, with a large mortgage and a considerable distance from our family.

All my life I had wanted a home that when my children came back to visit would feel like they were 'home'; a home that held all of their childhood memories. So in the end, everything did happen for a reason. The time we spent with Grace in our home was a blessing and I know she enjoyed dreaming right along with us of the home we could have all shared. She was always right there ready to jump in the car to go see the next house, and got just as excited as we did about the possibility. After Grace passed away, we took some time to mourn and then we went to work upgrading our home with an updated dream kitchen.

When the kids come to visit, it may look a little different, but it is home to all of us.

GOD Appeared

I remember the night well. It was a Monday evening, November 24, 2014. I was feeling deflated and overwhelmed. My heart was heavy with worry and I felt like I couldn't take much more. At that moment, all I wanted to do was cry. I needed to be by myself and just let it go. I went downstairs to sit in my quiet place where I could talk with God and get my composure back. As I was sharing with God my struggles and asking for Him to give me strength to deal with life's challenges and to take my worries away, I looked into the fireplace and saw His face literally appear on the wall of our pellet stove. At first I couldn't believe what I was seeing, and quickly I realized it was yet another sign.

The tears started to flow and I had to wipe my eyes in order to focus on the face I saw. It was clear and solemn, almost picture perfect to me. My first instinct was to grab my camera so I could capture the moment. I wanted to share this with my mother because I knew she too would recognize His face and the sign I received. He was looking down on me as if to say, "Do not worry, my dear. Give me your worries, and I will protect you." I know that He always has my back, so I took a deep breath and let it go to God.

Calm overcame my body and I felt such a sense of peace. God is always in control and wants the best for us. We just need to trust and give Him our burdens.

5

Inspiration Behind the Scenes

You know how sometimes you hear a song being played and, when it's over, you just can't seem to get the tune out of your head? Well, often times, that is exactly what our 'thoughts' do. Yes! That little voice inside that keeps repeating itself over and over is not to be taken lightly. It may be a thought that you have been contemplating, but for some reason you struggle with it to follow through. When that nudge begins to pull on your heart strings, just trust in God and believe He is directing your path.

I had been searching for years for just the right church where I could feel comfortable and at home. My best friend was also looking for a new church where she would feel compelled to go every week. We decided to meet at LifePoint Church, and both of us fell instantly in love with it. The contemporary service and the music hit my very soul. It was as if the Pastor was speaking directly to me. I felt something stir within, and I could just picture Mom up on that stage giving her testimony. I knew then that this church was going to play a role in our journey. I was elated to finally find my church. I actually look forward to Sundays now. After attending LifePoint Church, I was led on a spiritual journey that was unlike anything I'd ever experienced before.

Things began to happen that touched me greatly. Someone I mentioned the church to asked if I had heard of Paul Todd and if I followed his music. I had never heard of him, so I looked him up and fell in love with his music. I immediately downloaded a few of his songs and created my first spiritual music playlist.

The next day my husband was out of town on business where he had to take a test for a certification and conduct a presentation in front of a panel of judges. Needless to say, he was pretty stressed out. This was not his cup of tea and he didn't feel very positive about it. During my quiet time the morning of his presentation, as I prayed for God to give him the words, the confidence and professionalism to say what he needed, I received a sign that had me near tears. I told myself I needed to pray, yet I was still looking at Facebook and Twitter. I looked at the clock and again thought I needed to pray and still I went back to Facebook and Twitter. It was there that I saw a picture someone had posted of hands in the prayer position and "Ephesians 6:18-20" written beneath. I said, "Ok, that's my sign!" I instantly put down my iPad and said my prayers.

I had no idea what Ephesians 6:18-20 was about, but I said my prayers to ask God to give him the words to say so that he could confidently present his material. Afterward, I opened my Bible to Ephesians 6:18-19 and could not believe what I read. *"And pray in the Spirit on all occasions with all kinds of prayers . . . that whenever I speak, words may be given me so that I will fearlessly make known the mystery of the gospel . . ."* My prayer and the verses I read were basically one and the same. When he came home from his business trip, he said the words were put into his mouth and everything flowed flawlessly. He said he'd elaborated far more than he had practiced.

The week had already affected me enough spiritually that I knew this new church was my future. Then, Friday morning as I was having my quiet time, God spoke to me with such a strong voice that I was compelled to follow His lead. I felt I had no choice.

I had been receiving nudges for a while to document and share my signs from God. I had documented the signs that I'd received personally, and had even reached out to my Facebook friends and contacts in hopes of building a compilation of stories to put into a book, but none surfaced. I was disappointed and a little deflated, so when the idea to post on my community Facebook page had previously popped into my head, I brushed it off since my earlier attempt didn't work. But this particular morning when He spoke to me, His presence was strong, urging me to post on the community Facebook page asking for experiences with signs from God. This time, there was no hesitation. I immediately got up, without even finishing my prayers, and began composing my post. Once I clicked "post" on that message, I took a deep breath and just sat back. The rest was up to Him. What happened next was breathtaking and, to me, could only be God driven.

Facebook Post to the Sykesville Online Community
January 30, 2015

Good morning! I don't usually do this, but here goes . . . I'm working on a special project and would love to hear about the signs that God has given you that meant the most to you in your life. I've been reaching out in hopes of pulling together a compilation of stories and thought why not start in my own community! I would love to hear your stories! Feel free to PM me.

I drafted my post, re-read it once and said a prayer, then just let it go. I took a deep breath, waited, and wondered if anything would really come of it. It didn't take long until one special person started the trend of what became an overwhelming outpouring of love and support from total strangers.

I couldn't believe how fast the comments began to flow. It was hard to concentrate on anything other than the flood of Facebook pings and notifications that I was receiving. I should have known better and trusted Him the first time He tried to tell me to put a post on the site. The stories and comments were coming so fast I couldn't keep up. I was trying to capture comments and respond to them immediately in fear of losing the stories, or them somehow being deleted. I even put out a message to the admin for the site, asking them not to delete my post. I was assured it would not be deleted.

Having relieved my fear, I strategized a plan, and continued responding and documenting their stories. When I reached out to thank them, they shared even more stories and signs from God or their loved ones that had passed.

As the day flew by, I had the opportunity to chat with some amazing people—people that I look forward to meeting one day. Some of them offered to meet with me, some gave me their direct contact information and phone numbers, and everyone was thrilled to share their stories and be a part of this book!

That night I couldn't sleep. While I was lying in bed, all I could think about was how I was going to do this. I was so excited to start compiling all of the feedback. I finally gave in to my excitement and climbed out of bed. I was back on the computer at 3 a.m. dissecting all of the messages. The stories continued to pour in for a few days. I felt blessed for the new contacts and relationships I'd made. Out of respect for each person's privacy, I have left out last names, though none of them seemed to care, as they were just as excited as I to share their stories!

6

Sykesville Online Community

Is it a Coincidence, or Is There a Reason

As you've probably guessed by now, one of our favorite sayings is "Everything happens for a reason." We may think at first an experience is just a coincidence, but after you truly focus on all of the events and details that took place in order for that 'special' outcome to manifest you can't help but wonder if this is all part of His plan. If you hadn't been five minutes late, if you never went on that interview, if only you'd had a buyer for your house, things would be different. Fate would have changed. Every aspect of your day, year, life, would be different. God has a plan for us and every detail is planned out—in His time.

We are sharing the following stories as we received them. They have only been slightly edited as we felt they should be told in the words of those who have experienced them.

41

Valerie

In the past, I had been put through the mill when it came to relationships. The worse being an engagement that ended terribly, resulting in the money lost on the wedding that never happened. Years later, and very devoted to my Faith, I went on a Catholic Pilgrimage to Lourdes and Fatima with three of my best friends. We were all going thru something in our lives at that time. For me, I was older and praying that God and HIS Mother would help me find someone to put my life in order. On the way home during my flight from New York, I met a guy that was coming from Ireland after visiting his Grandparents. We both lived in Maryland, and he asked for my number. We ended up being total opposites, though he was the nicest and sweetest man I had ever met. We married a couple of years later, and will be celebrating 18 years of marriage this spring! I Believe, it was meant to be with us.

Anonymous

My husband and I were looking to purchase a new vehicle about two years ago and every car we test drove ended up breaking or something weird happened whenever my husband and I would switch seats to test drive. I would drive the car first and then he would test second. Without fail, when he was driving something happened. A tire went flat, or something under the hood went wrong. One of the wheels actually broke once. Another weekend, my husband, kids, and I just decided on a whim to stop at a local dealer. While my husband drove to the halfway mark, I prayed for God to give us a sign if this was the one. We switched and I drove back to dealer. Everything seemed great about it, except that when we got back to the dealer, I couldn't find my own car keys. I asked the dealer if I could drive back to the spot where we switched. Sure enough, there were my keys on the ground. That was my sign, another mishap during a switch. This car was not the one either! I told the dealer and my husband, and I think they thought I was a little crazy. I believe now that we didn't get those vehicles we test drove because they all would've been too small. You see, we found out a short time later, that we were expecting our third child. God knew that those cars would not have fit our family, and everything happened for a reason. I'm glad we listened.

Tammy

While we were on a camping trip, our son had a bad bicycle accident suffering with a possible brain injury. My husband, who was an emergency room nurse and didn't get excited easily, was driving way beyond our speedometer as he was so concerned about our son's injuries. While we were in the car, I couldn't pray because I was so close to tears. I started singing instead. The song that came to me was, "As the Deer Panteth for the Water." I asked God, why are you giving me this song? I don't even like this song! When we got to the hospital our son, who had been nearly unconscious, jumped out of the car and after observing him for an hour they sent him home. When we went to church the next Sunday, our Sunday school teacher, who knew nothing of what had happened on our vacation, was telling someone else a deer doesn't just go to water because it's thirsty, but to get away from its enemies. Obviously that has been one of my favorite songs ever since!

7

God Driven Agenda

When you are in the midst of a God driven agenda, you will know it. You'll feel it in your soul. The task at hand is all you will think about. Your frustration levels rise when you are not able to put the time and effort into His plan because that is all you truly want to do. We were put here on Earth to please God, and when we are blessed with the spirituality to accept Him and understand what it is He wants us to do, our desire to complete the task can consume us. At times, life may get in the way and deter us, yet He never gives up on us and continually nudges us back on track. When we can't see the next steps of His plan, do not fear, for He will lead us in the right direction and continue to give us signs.

Michele

God is constantly at work! When I started my drama ministry team, I fought it for a while, because I didn't want to do what God was clearly calling me to do. When I finally obeyed, I was overwhelmed with blessings, but it wasn't long before Satan stepped in. Things got very, very hard and my life completely changed! I was devastated by abuse, which elevated to federal prosecution levels. The constant barrage of aggressions had me believing I should take my life. At the last minute, God stopped me, and since then our ministry team has reached out to teens and young adults who struggle with self-destructive behavior, depression, and suicidal thoughts and actions. I'm now in a position to help others because I believe God uses rescued people to rescue people. I've been able to connect with young people across the nation and across the world to encourage them to seek God's grace & forgiveness. Sometimes, it's still hard. Old things still hurt and sometimes I get discouraged. A couple months ago I wasn't sure if I should continue with our team. It's hard to connect with other churches as an independent ministry team led by women. My team members are aging out, as our team is made of teens ranging between 14 and 19 years old. I wondered if God was preparing us for the end of our team. After all, it's His team to begin with and He can do as He pleases. I went to bed one night, crying, begging Him to show me if I should continue. I woke to a message from a man I hadn't heard from in years. He had videotaped one of our outreach events, and unbeknownst to me, he submitted the tape in an award program for media presentations and our team was awarded a bi-annual award for the best religious program! Even better yet, the panel of judges was a secular board, and exactly our audience! Within a couple of weeks, our team increased in size with younger teens and we were able to connect with an ecumenical association of 22 youth ministry groups, who have in turn expressed interest in a ministry partnership allowing us to perform for them on a semi-regular basis and perhaps travel with them to Central America! Is God good & faithful? Yes!! Always!! At times, we experience difficulties and trials we think may end us, or our work, but He is always there, painfully, powerfully, and perfectly in control! He is always working for our good and His glory, and I am so blessed to be submitted to His will!!

Linda

I retired several years ago and wanted to volunteer at the hospital. I didn't know what I would be able to do, but I truly felt like I was where I was meant to be. They assigned me to the Infusion Center; where patients come in for IV antibiotics, chemo, blood transfusions, etc. I had the best job in the world. After working all those years I was now responsible for passing out pillows, snacks and drinks. I knew I could handle that!

What a blessing it was to work in that unit. I met the most wonderful people, my patients. I felt like they were all part of my family. Some of them were grumpy, some happy, some too sick to be happy, but I loved them all. Of course, they loved me because I had goodies for them. There were three patients in particular that touched my heart and I knew God had sent them to me for a reason. The first, I'll call Nancy. She was there for transfusions because of a blood disease. We became such good friends. I would visit her at her apartment and bring her spaghetti, her favorite food. The second, I will call Candy who was 54 when we met and she was undergoing chemo. She had a son she absolutely adored and her biggest fear was leaving him. The third, I'll call Tim who always had his wife by his side. He was there for transfusions because of AML. He had 2 wonderful sons and several grandchildren, and you could just feel the love in that family.

I spent time with these three every week for almost a year watching as they felt better, felt worse, cried, laughed and fought a battle no one wants to fight . . . for their lives. We prayed for healing, easing their pain, a good night's sleep, every prayer imaginable in their situations even down to letting the nurse find a vein for the infusion. Even my husband, who is an excellent prayer warrior, came in and prayed with them when they needed him.

I went to see Nancy when she was moved to the University of Maryland Medical Center, but seeing her that way was more than I could emotionally handle. I left my husband in the room with her and went to the lobby to try to get it together. My husband prayed with her again but I was never able to go back in there. She went home to be with the Lord three days later.

I sat with Candy a few days before her 55th birthday and she confided that she wasn't afraid to die because she knew she was heaven bound, but she just wanted her son to be okay. Three days later God called her home on her 55th birthday.

I got the call that Tim had passed away in November that same year, which had been a terrible year of suffering for him. His wife knew, he too was heaven bound and that meant our "three musketeers" from the Infusion Center, were together again. One went home in August, one in September and the last one in November, all in the same year.

I thank God for blessing me by letting those three patients come into my life, even for the short time we had. They showed me what strength God gives, when we think we can't fight anymore.

Joy

This story goes back about 35 years, and I was in seventh grade. My mother was a stay-at-home mom and after she got her five children off to school, she always read the Bible and had her morning devotional time. One morning during this time, something told her to immediately pray for me. She felt that something was happening to me and I needed prayer. That same morning around the same time, my school bus had mechanical problems. The problem seemed to be extreme enough that the bus driver felt it was necessary for all the kids to immediately get off the bus. We were close enough to the school that we could see it, but the driver didn't want us to be in danger. I found out later that there was a problem with the gas tank, and the bus could have caught on fire. When I got home from school I told my mother what happened. A few years went by before she ever told me about her sudden need to pray for me. She had written everything down so she could remember the details and share it with me when the time was right. The story still gives me chills and brings tears to my eyes.

Terry

One afternoon a friend and I decided to go to Taco Bell. When we got there, for some reason, the door was locked and there was a sign on the door stating that the dining room will be closed until further notice. We decided to go to McDonalds, where we then encountered a Traveling Evangelist, named Ellis. We were sitting there eating when he walked by and noticed my books I had on the table: Heaven, by Randy Alcorn; Visions of Heaven, by Roberts Iaridon; and Journal of the Unknown Prophet, by Unknown. He immediately started up a conversation and we actually talked for over an hour about the things of God. I was so taken by him and caught up in such great conversation, that I asked him if he wanted to go to Bible Study with me in hopes of finding a place to stay. He was grateful, and jumped at the opportunity. After Bible Study, we dropped him back off at the same McDonalds. I felt an overwhelming sense of need placed on my heart, so strong that it could only be The Holy Spirit, urging me to ask if he was hungry. His eyes lit up and he said, "I could eat". I bought him what he wanted and we were on our way. I left feeling so blessed to have been able to help him not only find a place to stay, but also provide him with a meal and knowing that people out there do Believe and when people are driven together by God, only good things can happen! When I got home that night and opened my book, there was a $10 bill in my book. I don't mean I put it there and forgot, I mean it literally was not there before. God sees all that you are doing and remembers that which you have done for Him. I will remember this day forever and all the goodness and greatness of it belongs to God!

8

Asking For Signs

*For some yet-to-be believers, it is not uncommon for
them to ask for signs from God to help them begin their
spiritual journey and build their relationship with Him.
At the same time, those who believe also continue to
pray and ask for signs from God to help lead us on His
path so that we can please Him by fulfilling His desire
for us. Often we will even ask our loved ones who have
already passed to be with the Lord for signs from them
that they are okay. When these prayers are answered,
and He clearly provides us with the signs we need, it is
mind-boggling. Once we begin to recognize even the
smallest of signs, our spirituality continually blossoms.
Opening up our hearts and souls to recognizing many
more signs.*

Cindy

Before my husband was diagnosed with ALS, he coached for our boy/girl set of twins in all of their sports: baseball, softball, football, and basketball. One year, the Boys Basketball Team gave him a signed basketball as a coach's gift. As we came into the garage from the team party, I asked if he wanted me to toss it in the ball bin. He said, "No! I'm holding onto this." He kept it on top of his armoire and every once in a while, he'd pick it up and look over it, reading all the names. I thought it was cute how he really appreciated and cherished that ball. It really is reflective of his character and how much he thought of the kids he coached. Individual goals came first to him, and then team goals. He really focused on each player to bring out their best. If they made a basket for the first time, nobody was happier for that child than Coach Tim. Tim fought for two and half years with ALS before ALS ended his battle. Before he passed, we talked a lot about him giving me a sign, so I'd know he was okay. He said that he would. After he passed, we had several odd things happen when the kids and I were together and we'd all stop and look at one another, then one would say, "Daddy?" I talked to him and said I felt like I was being greedy, because I "think" he's already given me signs. But, I needed a sign that would prove, without a doubt, he was okay and one where I couldn't just explain it away. Well, I got it!

After months of sleeping on the couch, next to his hospital bed in our living room, it was finally time for me to move back into our bedroom. I struggled so much with that because it was "our" room. I decided to completely redo it and make it "my" room, which included selling all of the furniture. It was while I was in the midst of clearing stuff out. Well, you know when you clear things out, it always looks worse before it gets better. I had everything pulled out in the middle of the room. If you were walking in there, you barely had enough room to carefully place your foot in between all the clutter. The ball though, was still sitting on top of the armoire. It had been there for a couples years and had lost quite a bit of air. Miraculously though, it fell off the armoire and, somehow, made it across the room, through the many obstacles on the floor, passed all of the clutter of stuff blocking the door, out the door, into the hallway, and then turned sharply before bouncing down the stairs, one by one. I don't like to use the word bounced because, like I said, the ball was somewhat deflated and it was as if it bounced in slow motion, very methodically, one step at a time. When it reached the bottom, it just stopped. When I heard the bouncing, I looked over and watched that basketball make its way down the stairs where our dog ran over sniffing like crazy, something he'd never done before. As I picked it up, and started hugging it, I began to cry and reassured him that I had not planned to get rid of his ball! It was bizarre, and without a doubt, a sign that definitely couldn't be explained away. A memory I will treasure forever that always makes me smile and believe!!!

Stacey

My father tragically passed away from a brain trauma in July of 2013. We were very close and he adored his grandchildren. Just before Christmas that year, our first without my dad, I was sitting alone in our family room thinking about how much I missed him. When, all of a sudden, one of the recordable ornaments on our Christmas tree went off. It was one that had a picture of my daughter on Santa's lap and the recording was her singing "Here Comes Santa Claus," that ends with her saying, "Merry Christmas". The only way to turn it on was to push a button on the top. I walked over to the tree and asked my dad if he was the one who turned it on. I asked him to do it again if he was there with me. I waited a few seconds and it didn't go off again, so I started to turn and walk away. Just as I did, the ornament went off again. It is the only time it ever happened, and I know my dad was letting me know he was with me.

Sandy

Many years ago for Christmas I bought my mom a large suitcase from JC Penney. They had just started making the kind with wheels on them, and I had asked her if she wanted any matching pieces, but she said, "No, just the suitcase was fine for now". The year she passed away, my husband and I went to Key West for the holidays. I wanted to be as far away as possible of any reminders of Christmas without my mom. I went to Marshalls shopping (yes they have them in Key West), and low and behold there was a matching travel bag like the suitcase I had given my mom. Now mind you it had been several years since I had given her that luggage!! A few years later, we went back to Key West and mom's suitcase was too big to take as they were starting to crack down on the size and weight restrictions of baggage. So I ordered myself a Leopard print one on line. When I went back to try to get some matching pieces they were nowhere to be found. I said a little prayer to my mom like "Hey, if you can help me out with this luggage situation . . ." So I go back to Marshalls in Key West while on vacation, and guess what . . . there on the shelf is practically the identical Leopard print luggage to match my suitcase, and it was crazy cheap to boot!! I bought three matching pieces!! As I walked out of the store, something on the ground caught my eye. I started to walk past it, but somehow felt compelled to turn back around and see what it was.

As I picked up the little gift tag on the ground, it said "To: Sandi, From: Santa". Now granted, I spell my name with a "y" not an "i", but still this was just too much of a coincidence. My mom would, often times, sign the gift tags "From: Santa". Today, the gift tag is in a picture frame, along with the last photo of the two of us. Little gifts from Heaven!!!

Sherry

My daughter was diagnosed with Neuroblastoma in March of 2007. During her first weeks in the hospital, we were in a room at the end of the hall when we noticed a lady bug (known for good luck). I took this lady bug out of her room and placed it near the window at the end if the hall. During her many months of treatment, we would periodically be assigned to this room, and each and every time we would see that ladybug. My daughter was sent home in November of 2007 with Hospice, and she passed away in December of 2007. On the day of her funeral, I locked myself in my bathroom praying and crying in pain. I then decided that if I did not go to the funeral, it would not happen. I prayed for her to give me a sign, make me go and do this. It was then that I noticed something buzzing near my head. I looked up, and there was one ladybug crawling down my bathroom wall. It was the sign I needed. She gave me the strength to do what I feared the most.

Cindy

My grandmother passed away in 1992 and there was a song out at the time that always made me think of her. Fifteen years later, I was shopping for party supplies for my five year old twins' birthday party, when I felt someone over my shoulder. When I turned to look, there was no one around me. I then felt it again, and it was even closer, as if someone was right there on my shoulder. The feeling was so strong it practically took my breath away. I couldn't believe it, but I knew someone was there with me, so I actually whispered, "I know someone is with me. Give me a sign so I know who it is." Just then, that fifteen year old song came on in the store.

9

Signs From Heaven

It's awe inspiring knowing that your loved one has passed through the Golden Gates of Heaven. I know many nights I've worried and prayed that my loved ones come to terms with their spirituality and are able to build a strong relationship with God. I understand that you can't push God on anyone. It is up to them and God. When the time is right, I pray it will happen. When your loved ones have accepted God as their savior and you know they have made it to Heaven, it gives you such peace knowing they are safe in the arms of Jesus when their time on this Earth is done. It gets even better when, after they pass, you recognize signs that can come only from Heaven and God reassuring us that all is well.

Rene

When my husband died, my sister-in-law was in the room with me. He died on a rainy October day. Despite the rain, when he took his last breath, the rays of the sun covered his bed and slowly left the room. It was like a scene from an old movie. I never told my sister-in-law I saw this, as I figured she would think I was crazy. It wasn't until about twelve years later when we were together, and the subject accidently came up, when we realized that we both saw the rays of sun cover his bed that day and we are still in awe!

Matthew

On October 9, 2012, my parents were involved in a car wreck that took my mother's life while on vacation at the Northern rim of the Grand Canyon. At the request of my father, two days after the accident, my wife, my father, and I relived my mother's last day on earth. We started at the site of the accident, and it had been raining all day which did not help with the emotions flying around. Before I got out of our rental car, I prayed and asked three things: 1) that the rain would stop, 2) that it would snow (My mother loved snow), and 3) that I would see a rainbow. As I finished my quick prayer and I opened that car door, the rain stopped immediately. The sun was out for the remainder of the day while we relived the last day of my mother's life. That night we received a dusting of snow, and for the next weeks I was looking for my rainbow to no avail. On the day of my mother's funeral, I walked outside to see what the day was like, and behind my house was a double rainbow.

Kim

My mother passed away back in May 2014. The day of her funeral, Saturday, May 24th, was a beautiful sunny day that I will never forget. After the funeral, out of nowhere, a little storm came up and blew through while we were all sitting on the screened-in back porch. Shortly after the storm, we looked out the back of the house, and there was a rainbow pointing directly at the cemetery. We knew that was a sign from my mom. Everyone got out their cell phones and cameras and started taking lots of pictures.

Mae

My brother passed away ten years ago in April. When he was dying, I told my mother to tell him he could go. As hard as it was for her to tell him it was okay to go, she did. It was at that very moment when he took his last breath. Just as he took his last breath, the sun shone bright in the sliding glass door. The music playing softly in the background, got louder and louder, and I got chills up my spine.

Dianne

I had always agonized over whether my parents were "true" believers. The day we buried my mother was a very rainy, dark, and grey December day. In the little English Chapel, as we were singing a hymn, my mind was saying to God *"I do hope she is with you Lord".* At that very moment, a ray of sunshine shone down through the stained glass window and rested on the open bible that laid on the lectern right in front of me. Given the fact that there was no sun at any time during that entire week, it had to be a sign from above. A sense of peace came over me and all I could do was smile. I had my answer!

10

Loved Ones

Speak to Us from Heaven

We've shared many signs received from God letting us know that our loved ones are with Him. And even though we may know they are true believers, we still can't help but wonder . . . "Are they with God? Are they okay? Are they watching over us?" It's normal for us to look for signs to reassure us they are okay, they are with God, and that ever-lasting life is a reality. Then that moment comes when you receive a sign from them that proves beyond a shadow of doubt that they are safe and their spirit is always with us.

Stacy

My dad passed away in November of 2013. Three months later, I was cleaning out and packing up my desk for an office move and found a card he had sent me years and years ago. I didn't even remember I had it. It said "Dear Stacy, I miss you. Love, Dad".

Jessie

I just lost one of my closest, lifelong friends in a car accident last week. We had a bathroom joke going between us since we were kids. At work the other day, I went to use the staff bathroom which is a one person bathroom and when I knocked, nobody answered. I tried opening the door and couldn't get in because it was locked. I waited a few minutes and nobody came out, so I tried the door again. Still it was locked, and I couldn't open it. I knocked again, and said, "Is anyone in there?" I then tried the door handle again, and it opened right up. I had been praying he'd give me a sign he was ok, and it would be just like him to play a joke like that!

Jean

My sister, Mary, is petrified of the thought that souls come back and are around you. My sister, Michelle, is always looking for signs of people surrounding her. I am a prankster and so was my dad, Opa. When Opa was dying, I said, "Let's pull a joke on my sister. Tell her you will send pennies from heaven." Well, I asked my sister, "Have you found any pennies lying around?" She said, "No". I asked if dad had told her he'd send pennies from Heaven and her response was simply, "No". Anyway, months later as I was vacuuming my house to sell, there were pennies all over the house! I found them in corners and under furniture, and they were all dated the year he died. I guess the joke was on me.

Rachael

My grandmother had just had surgery on her shoulder and was going through the healing process. She loved dogs and has had many over the years. When my mom and I went to visit her in the hospital, all she could talk about was that when she got better she was going to get a Yorkie. Well, much to our surprise, my grandmother never fully recovered from her surgery. One thing led to another, and it was a short time later when she was diagnosed with ovarian cancer and only given a matter of weeks to live. Her untimely death took my family by complete surprise and rocked my whole world. I was so distraught. All I could do was cry. A few weeks after she passed away, I heard barking at my door. I looked out, and there was a Yorkie sitting on my front porch. When I opened the door, it jumped right into my arms when I leaned down to pet it. It took me a while, but I did finally find the owner down the street. I had lived there for eight years and never had seen this dog before. Then later that day, I was sitting in the doctor's waiting room when a commercial came on the TV and I saw yet another Yorkie. It was that day and those Yorkie's that made me realize it was my grandmother's way of letting me know . . . she was better!!

11

Dreams Speak to Us

Have you ever been fortunate enough to have a loved one come to you in a dream? Have you ever had a dream that was a premonition of what was to come; a warning from God or a loved one? These dreams can change our lives when we listen and believe. They can give us a sense of peace in knowing that our loved ones are well and are watching out for us. You may think sometimes it is crazy to follow-up on a dream; but afterwards when you look back at the events that took place and how it impacted your life, you can't help but recognize the signs from God and/or your loved one and feel blessed, and so thankful.

Sharon

I lost my father one year ago this month. During his illness my sister was dying from breast cancer, and my mom had two collapsed disks in her lower spine along with three other herniated disks. She was unable to get to my Father daily to advocate for him, so my younger sister and I did it almost every day, splitting shifts for a year and a half. A week before he passed he visited me in a dream. He grabbed my hand and kissed my cheek. I can still feel his breath on my cheek and the sound of my hair moving past my ear. I was concerned about something that represented him having fallen to the ground. In my dream he stopped me and said, "Don't get tangled up in that." I reached again, and again, he stopped me. Then music began playing so loudly in my head that it woke me up. It was Louis Armstrong, 'It's a Wonderful World'. Lying there awake, I could still hear the music. I am asking myself, *"Why this song? Why so loud?"* My sister and I planned the entire funeral service. I had requested that song to be played at the end of the service, without discussing it with my mom. When she heard that song, she began to cry and I could see how it rattled her. I asked her why it upset her so much and she told me it was her and my dad's favorite 'secret' song. I was stunned, and had no idea. Since then, at various times, my iPad spontaneously plays his favorite Frank Sinatra songs. On New Year's Eve, it played "Angel Eyes" which begins with, "Hey drink up, all you people. Order anything you see. Have fun, you happy people. The drink and the laughs are on me. Try to think that loves not around, still it's uncomfortably clear. My old heart isn't gaining ground because my angel eyes aren't here." I have constantly been amazed by the songs that spontaneously play as they are always meaningful at the time.

Andrea

Almost two years ago, my son, Aidan, died. He was almost nine at the time and his younger brother, Chris, was four. Chris, like the rest of us, was extremely upset and trying really hard to understand. One morning, Chris came in and said he had a dream about Aidan. In his dream they were at what he thought was a beach, except that the sand was glittery. He then said there was a very tall woman who was also glittery. He said that she took Aidan and Chris by the hands and swung them in circles and that Aidan laughed. In his dream, he said Aidan was also running around and laughing; when normally, he was wheelchair bound and cognitively disabled. I really believe he dreamed of an Angel, who was showing him that his brother was now okay and no longer needed his wheelchair!

Cindy

It was when my son and daughter, who are twins, were 3 months old, that I had a dream about a medical emergency with my daughter. As soon as I got up, I pulled out papers from the hospital folder on how to perform infant CPR. I carefully read them, while practicing on a baby doll. When the twins awoke, I began nursing and my daughter stopped breathing. I immediately started CPR and she started to cry. The papers were literally right next to me on the bed! I was able to remain calm and do what I had to do. Turns out she had a severe form of acid reflux and refluxed at the same time she swallowed which shut off her airway. The doctor said this easily could've happened in her sleep. If not for that dream, I don't know if I would've been successful in saving her.

One night when I was somewhere between the ages of 10-12, I had a dream that God was the size of a giant and lifted up the roof of my house. He peered down at me and started talking. The only thing, was that I couldn't hear what he was saying. I kept saying, "I can't hear you! I can't hear you!" The next day, my parents went out for a couple of hours and I was watching my two younger brothers. We decided to have ice cream so we took a glass jar of hot fudge and put it in the microwave and set it for two minutes. When it was finished, my little brother reached up to pull the glass jar out of the microwave. At the last minute, I decided to do it myself. Or did God, put the thought in my mind? Of course, none of us were anticipating how hot it was going to be. I dropped the jar and the fudge hit my leg giving me a pretty bad burn. It was then I realized that if my little brother would have pulled it out, he was at the right height that the extremely hot fudge would have gotten right in his eyes, possibly blinding him. I was thankful that I was the one who got hurt and I have always wondered if that dream was warning me to help my brother.

Chanda

Eight years ago was the first Christmas without my dad. After shopping early Black Friday morning that year, I came home with my hands full of gifts. I was tired, so I decided to lay on the couch downstairs and I fell asleep. While I was asleep, my husband came down and kissed me on the cheek. Awhile later when I awoke and went upstairs, my husband asked, "Did you break the bank?" as if I'd been gone all day. I smiled and said, "You know I was down stairs asleep on the couch, you came down and kissed me on my cheek and left." He said, "No, I did not. I just woke up." Till this day, all I can think is it was my dad telling me he loves me and he is ok. I just wish I could get more visits like that.

Sharon

One night, I had a dream where Conan visited me. He was lying at the top of stone steps, next to a beautiful iron gate, and beyond the gate, was a beautiful garden. I was rattled by how authentic it seemed, looked, and felt. It made me feel like he was telling me he was waiting for me. On my 40th Birthday, my husband presented me with a special gift of which he had no idea what he was giving me. It was a collectable painting by Thomas Kincaid, whom I admired greatly, but was not a collector. I was stunned to see this image without my Conan, because it was the exact location where I saw him in my dream sitting at the top of those stone steps, next to a beautiful iron gate, and beyond the gate, was the same beautiful garden! I was literally paralyzed in awe, and I still cry when I look at this painting. Animals do have souls!

Jessica

My daughter was three years old at the time and woke me up at 4:45am one morning covering her ears, and screaming, "The bikes, the bikes, their hurting my ears!" I finally got her calmed down and was trying to figure out what type of bikes she was talking about. I thought maybe like ATV's because we lived near a farm that had some riding around once in a while. Fifteen minutes later I actually heard what she was describing and it did sound like ATV's or motor bikes. A split second later, I felt something hit the house so hard that it knocked things over in the bathroom. Meanwhile, my daughter is in hysterics still screaming that the bikes are hurting her ears. It was actually an earthquake. I couldn't believe it. It was like she had a premonition in her sleep. We talked about it again, and she said God told her it was coming.

12

When Angels Are Sent to Us

Many have been fortunate to have family come to them in their dreams or receive signs from heaven letting them know they are okay, but it's not just family that reaches out to us. God often sends complete strangers to us in time of need to help us through difficult times, help us recognize and come to terms with something we've been dealing with, or just simply intervene where needed. These angels typically appear just in the nick of time and walk out of our lives when their job is done. Read how Arlene Garrett, the co-author, shares one of these stories with us.

Arlene Garrett

I was in the hospital at the time suffering from a broken pelvis, a fractured sacrum, and a broken nose all from being thrown from a horse. I was in excruciating pain and afraid of the effects the pain medication may have on me when an angel came to visit me in the middle of the night. Several years before this accident I had experienced my nervous breakdown as I've spoken of. During that time, I was administered many different medications that altered my abilities to function, which rendered me incapacitated and hospitalized on several occasions for periods of time. With all of that behind me and starting my new life, it was clear to me that medications for anxiety were not healthy for me and I was determined to stay clear. For this reason, the thought of just taking pain medication scared me beyond belief. I didn't want to revert back to relying on any medications, whether it was for pain or anxiety, and I certainly didn't want to suffer another breakdown. The more I worried about this, on top of the pain I was in, the more it bothered me to the point that I was starting to have panic attacks that I couldn't get under control. When I told the nurse what I was feeling, she left my room for a few minutes and came back with a paper bag for me to breathe into, in an attempt to calm the anxiety down. Unfortunately, this exercise was not helping me and the panic attacks continued. I remember feeling extremely fearful, and began to pray out loud for God to help me. As I lay there in bed, I continually prayed for God to help get me through this, and I was able to calm down some. During my breakdown, it was He who saved me through a miraculous healing, and I knew he would get me through this, too. Shortly after this episode that evening, sometime after midnight with visiting hours well over, a lady came into my room, walked over to my bed, and held my hand. I was surprised by her visit at that hour of the night, and I distinctly remember how angelic her expression seemed to be as she reassured me that I was not going to get sick again. She told me that she was there to tell me I would be okay and my breakdown was all behind me. After a while, she patted my hand and calmly said I was going to be alright now. Then she slowly turned and walked out of the room. She'd calmed me down with just her presence. It was then that I took a deep breath and gave a sigh of relief. A peaceful calm came over my body and I knew that I would get through this with the help of God. My anxiety had subsided.

When the nurse came in shortly after, I asked her, "Who was the woman that was just in my room?" The nurse looked at me, very doubtful, with a strange expression. I explained that she was in plain street clothes and was not a nurse or doctor. The nurse said, "Oh, sweetheart, no one was here. You must have been dreaming. Visiting hours have been over for a long time." However, I know without a doubt that she was there, and I was awake. God sent an angel to get me through that night and relieve my fears.

Natalie

Without fail, whenever I encountered a crossroad, He led me. He directed my steps, providing a road map pointing in the direction I should go. He always sent someone to show Himself to me, through the time and care they displayed. These strangers and acquaintances were always there for me the second I would seriously doubt His existence. My childhood was really painful. It really was, but God did not leave me alone. He sent angels to keep me strong and to always believe.

Connie

My sister had passed away from cancer three years earlier, but her official cause of death was a pulmonary embolism! Then one day I was admitted to the hospital with pulmonary embolisms and I too was diagnosed with Lupus. This day had been pretty crazy, and I hadn't been feeling well and was extremely short of breath. I was in the shower getting ready for a doctor appointment and I passed out. I came to and started screaming for my mom. My dad had to break the bathroom door and pull me out of the shower. The ambulance showed up and took me to the ER. After many tests, they found my chest riddled with blood clots. Later that night, after finally getting a room and being hooked up to IV's, heart monitors, and oxygen, I was finally alone and it was quiet. The enormity of what I was dealing with finally dawned on me, and I couldn't help but think of my sister. I started to pray. I was so scared and only 28 years old. Not long after, a wonderful nurse, who knew my mom, came in and sat with me. She just held my hand and let me cry. She was such a comfort to me that night and quietly gave me strength. I believe God sent her to me for a reason.

Kim

When I was fairly new to nursing, I was taking care of a 16-year old boy who had been shot. As I was caring for him, we discussed lots of things. Then, he asked me if I had accepted the Lord Jesus Christ into my life. I was naive (ok, stupid) and said, "Of course I have, I'm catholic." He looked at me, in pain, and grabbed my hand and held it. He said, but have you really accepted Him as your Savior? I looked blankly at him (I guess he figured out I was clueless), and asked if we could pray together. I said yes. Here was this child, not much younger than I at the time, praying for my soul. He asked if I was ready to accept Jesus Christ as my Savior. I said, "Yes!" From that day forward, my relationship with God has been different, good, and consistent. I feel Him constantly, and I find myself getting little reminders constantly. I will forever be grateful to this child, while during his own suffering, he prayed for me. I don't know what happened when he was discharged, but I believe in my heart that Jesus spoke through him that day.

Jean

I have a 4 year old granddaughter that actually sees her deceased grandfather. I know it sounds wacky, but she never met him. He had died of cancer, and his face was scarred. There were no photos of him this way, yet she described who she was playing with and she mentioned his face. There have been lots of instances when children are blessed with seeing angels, and on this day, I truly believe my granddaughter was playing with her deceased grandfather.

Rene

This past October when my phone had issues, I went to Verizon in DC. They ordered me a new phone and while headed home I went to call my daughter to let her know I would be very late. Well, my phone would not work, and the only number it would dial was 611-Verizon. So I called and asked them to call my daughter and relay the msg. The lady from Verizon wanted to try to reset my phone and I told her I was in DC on the highway and was not going to pull over. She understood and then called my daughter and gave her the message. She then said that she felt God telling her she needed to stay on the phone with me until I got home. While I was still on the phone with the lady from Verizon, I saw a deer in the middle of the road as I crossed over Rte. 108. I slowed down from 55mph to 25mph, and moved to the shoulder. As I was still slowing, the deer ran into my car, hit my front drivers quarter panel, slid up my hood and then up my windshield, went airborne, slammed down on the roof of my car right behind my sunroof before it slid down my rear window and off my car. My car was not drivable. She asked me where I was and then called my daughter again and told her about the accident. Another woman witnessed it and everyone said that had I not slowed down, I would be dead. My car was totaled. Insurance estimated over $8K in damage on the exterior before they quit counting. The Verizon

Customer Representative was my Guardian Angel that day!

Beth

My great aunt passed away recently, after having a massive stroke and being in the hospital for over a week. She communicated with her kids, but never opened her eyes. The doctor came to check on her and said, "Vi, why won't you open your eyes?" She said, "It is too beautiful." Many times throughout that week she would tell her kids the people that she was seeing that had already passed on to be with the Lord. I believe the angels were there with her comforting her in her last days.

13

The Gift of Children

Just as God has sent us angels to help us cope or get through difficult situations, he also brings us little miracles that we are fortunate enough to recognize as such. Many times, the miracle of birth comes shortly after losing a loved one who has gone to be with the Lord. Then, when we look into the faces of these precious gifts from God, we know their legacy lives on. These bundles of joy take away our pain and sorrow and help us to realize the circle of life and God's presence through it all.

Rachael

My husband and I had been trying for years to conceive our first child. My grandmother wanted nothing more than to hold her first great-grandchild in her arms. Unfortunately, in January my grandmother went to be with the Lord very unexpectedly. It took the entire family by complete surprise and totally shook our world. I had just begun investigating IVF and the costs associated to see if we could swing this. I had started my prenatal vitamins and was going through acupuncture as a means to calm my stress and prepare me for this journey, when we learned my grandmother had ovarian cancer. It was so progressive that she was only given weeks to live; all I could think about was that she would never get to meet my baby. It was a month later when I was inseminated, and shortly thereafter we learned that I was officially pregnant. The day my second Trimester began was my grandmother's birthday, and the day we planned to announce we were expecting our first child! Through all of the emotional ups and downs of my grandmother's death, I know that her spirit will live on in my child. If she is a girl, she will be named after my grandmother!

Connie

My daughter was born August 2005, and my dad passed away the next month. If not for having her to keep me busy and knowing she needed me, I don't know how I would have gotten through that time. I was totally a 'Daddy's Girl', and am so grateful he was able to meet my daughter before he passed away. I have two pictures of them together that I will cherish forever. Five years later when my son was born in 2010, I could see so much of my dad in him. I miss him so much!

Jean

My husband Joe, walked out after 30 years of marriage. Our Anniversary was March 20th. The year after my husband left, my grandson was born on March 20th. God turned a day I would begin to dread, into a new day of celebration! Ironically enough, He turned another day of mourning into a day of celebration when my second grandson was born on the date of my father's death. God always has a way of turning bad things into good!

Brenda

My first grandchild was born in June 2007 and I lost my mom in August 2007. I have always believed that God sent me a grandson to help ease the pain of losing my mom so unexpectedly. I'm so glad that my mom got to meet her first great grandchild. Since then, God has blessed me with two more grandchildren.

Debbie

When my son was two years old, he went on to be with the Lord. He was born on November 7th and died on March 9th. I hated those two days. Every year I was reminded me of his birth, and of his death, and would dread every anniversary. Many years later, my first grandchild was born on November 7th, and my second grandchild was born on March 9th. I truly believe that God chose these birthdays for my grandchildren in order to bring joy back into my life on these two days.

Chelsea

My son was born in February of 2013. Unexpectedly, my mother passed away seven weeks later at 43 years old. I think God gave me my son to help me find strength after her passing.

14

When Prayers are Answered

There's nothing better than having your prayers answered by God. It reaffirms our beliefs. What we have to realize, though, is that even God's unanswered prayers are blessings. Blessings that we may not recognize right away, but in the end when we look back, we realize He has a better plan for us. Things happen for a reason—we just need to hold onto that and trust that he has a plan.

Natalie

God gave me amazing children, one of which is an absolute prayer warrior. Joshua is only nine years old, but his prayers are powerful and he gets it. He is my amazing boy, who is dyslexic, but has an IQ of 130. Reading is a struggle for him, yet he is a problem solving genius! I don't see dyslexia as a disability for him; his problem solving is impeccable, and his reading is coming along slowly. When he prays, his prayers are answered. I believe his faith is simple; and, for his issues, he finds solutions. He makes the solutions make sense to anyone, not just himself. Faith is supposed to be pure and simple. People make it difficult to understand. This is why I believe his prayers get answered.

Elvina

I have always believed in God and Christ, but I do not go to church anymore. I have gone to different ones over the years, and I more or less move to the beat of my own drum. I was living in Michigan, and was moving up North to be closer to my sister. I was a single mom and was with my 4-year old little boy, Anthony, while we were driving back home to collect more of my stuff when my car blew out a tire. I was raised by my father and I knew how to change a tire, but when I popped the trunk open, I had no Jack. This happened back in the day, before cell phones. I was in the middle of nowhere, no homes, no nothing. About 30 minutes back from where I came was a little town, and about a 30 minute drive ahead was a bigger town. It normally isn't hot in Michigan, but on this day it was 95 degrees outside. I got back in the car, left the trunk up in hopes someone would notice and stop. In an attempt to keep Anthony busy, I got a board game out of the trunk that I happened to have from the move. Car after car after car drove by us. I was at the point where I thought I am going to have to take this baby and walk. Instead, I asked God as I sat there sweating from the heat, *"Where are all the good people, Lord?"* and within five minutes, a white station wagon pulled up with four elderly people in it. I asked if they had a jack, and he told me he was afraid his jack wouldn't work on my car. He said he would drive down the road and call a tow truck to come help. I told him I didn't have any money, and asked if he could just call the police for me. He got out his wallet and gave me a twenty dollar bill. I told him I didn't want to take it, but he insisted. I asked for his address so I could send it back to him, and he told me to just help someone else out if I see them in a bad way. He drove off and returned a short time later. He told me that he called a tow truck and the police. I thanked him again and returned to my car and waited. In the meantime, I had three people stop and ask me if I needed help, and I told them help was on the way. Then one man pulled up and gave me a jug of water and asked if I needed help. I told him the same, that help was on the way, and he left the water with me. The policeman got there before the tow truck driver, so he pulled up behind me and sat in his car and waited for the tow truck. When the tow truck pulled in front of me, a young father jumped out with his two boys about nine and ten years of age. He had seen Anthony in the car, and told his boy to run back to the truck and get that little guy a soda. He then proceeded to change my tire. When I asked him how much I owed him, he said, "Nothing, don't worry about it." I said, "But, you don't understand. The man that called for me, he gave me money to pay you." He said, "Next time you're around, just stop at my station for your gas. That's good enough." I went home overwhelmed, full of joy and tears, going over the events of the day. God is real. God is great. He has been there on several occasions and even in such a powerful way as this; but this day, changed the way I see and talk to God. It changed my life forever.

Fast forward to when my son was a senior, I was taking him and his friend to school. It was cold and dark out when I turned the corner and saw a car on the side of the road. I pulled over, which was very unlike me in this situation without my husband with me. My son even said, "Mom, your stopping?" I said, "Yes, what if that was you?" The young man walked up to the window and said, "Oh thank you so much. Nobody would stop! I have been waving cars down for twenty minutes." I asked what was wrong and he said, "My car broke down and my sister is in there with her baby. Can I use your cell phone to call my Mom?" So, I gave him my phone. After he called, I asked if he was ok and needed anything else. He said no, and that mom was on her way and he thanked me. As I drove away that day, and still now, it makes me cry thinking back to the events that took place years ago, and knowing that I had paid it forward to the right person.

Mary Ellen

When I was pregnant with my second son, now 13, I almost lost him a few times in the early part of the pregnancy. I prayed all of the time to Saint Therese of Lisieux, as I did in my first pregnancy, because I was so afraid of losing him after a miscarriage. When my first son was born five weeks early and perfectly healthy on her feast day of October 1st, I knew it wasn't a coincidence! So, in my second pregnancy I prayed almost exclusively to her. People say that sometimes, she gives a 'sign' that she is listening and all will be well. That sign is the smell or sight of roses when it's unexpected. Well, two things happened. The first sign I received was one day in late November when I was in the yard playing with my toddler. A ball got near a part of the yard that we didn't do much with. There, under some leaves, was a blooming pink rose. I have no idea how the plant got there. I'd never seen it before. The second sign was during an early sonogram to see if the heartbeat was there, and while I was in the waiting room, I smelled the fragrance of roses - like someone had on perfume or there was a bouquet nearby. I looked around and asked people around me, do you smell that? Do you smell roses? Nobody else could smell them and they looked at me funny. But, I smelled them and I knew then, that everything would be ok.

Stacie

My dog is currently in late stage kidney failure. To say we are very close is an understatement. We spend every day, all day, together cuddling on the couch since I've been sick the last few years, but especially the last six months. The other night I asked for prayers on my Facebook page because she had not been doing well for about a week. She was hardly eating, and I had to carry her down the steps because her back legs were too weak. After I asked for prayers, I asked God to please show me or let me know somehow whether it was time to make that tough decision to assist her in leaving me. A few hours later she got up out of nowhere and used her steps to get off the couch. She hadn't done this in about a week. I was elated and took her outside where she started happily walking almost too fast through the snow, with her tail wagging the whole way! I kept taking pictures of her because I couldn't believe what I was seeing! I kept saying thank you God over and over.

Linda

My mother and her baby sister had a falling out probably 30 years ago. The anger and resentment seemed unbreakable. Even when my grandmother passed away, it was uneasy at best. At that time the feud spilled out over other members of the family including me. I couldn't be her friend if she didn't love my mom. As the years passed, I ran into my aunt several times when her brother was very ill and hospitalized. As the meetings became more frequent, the tension eased and we started to talk more. I would drop little statements about what my mom was doing, but she expressed no interest. I prayed for God to soften both of their hearts if His will was to heal this relationship.

I started talking to my aunt on the phone and would tell my mom when we spoke. She wasn't receptive initially, but I kept praying and knew that God was working on both of them. Several months later I told my aunt about my mother's health and told her that I had been praying for both of them because I think they would never forgive themselves if one of them went home to be with the Lord without resolving their differences. I told her she didn't know how long she would have her big sister and thought she should try calling mom.

I told Mom what I had done and she seemed somewhat pleased that she may hear from her 'kid sister', as she called her. I kept praying and, when I spoke to each of them, I would relay what the other was doing and where they were going, anything that would keep their sister on their minds. After a short while, my aunt called my mom and they spoke briefly and agreed to keep in touch. That was about two years ago and now they speak every week and have even gone to visit each other. God brought them back together by showing them the love they thought was gone forever.

Jessica

I just found out I was pregnant on a Monday this past August. That Saturday before I found out, I had just sat down on the couch when my daughter comes over to me, kneels down, and touches my belly and says, "Hi, baby boy." This pretty much freaked me out, but I blew it off saying, "I thought you always wanted a sister?" She went on to say that she didn't care and that either boy or girl was good. I laughed and told her to leave me alone. A couple days later when we found out that we were expecting, she was so happy she was crying and said that she had been praying for this. I told her next time she prays for something like this to please talk to me about it first. She is seven years old and I'm due in April, and . . . it's a Boy!

Linda

My first marriage ended when my son was young so I found myself in that position we never expect; the single mom. I was raised in a Christian home but had strayed away from the church for a long time before the divorce. I can truly say that no matter what I did or what happened in my life, I still knew when it was time to pray for the only help I could ask for privately. I was too prideful to go to my family or friends, I was afraid of their judgment. When my son became a teenager the struggles began. I think the school had me on speed dial. It was all stupid things that hurt him, not others, thank God. After graduation, I experienced a new side of him, full of lies and deceit. A side I never would have expected. I kept praying for help and knew that, in God's time, He would help me.

My current husband was having medical problems so I asked my son to stay with his dad until I could get my husband back on his feet. He was very angry because he felt like I was kicking him out, but I knew I could not handle what he was doing while getting my husband through recovery. Unfortunately, he chose to stay at his dad's even when I asked him to come home; I had too many rules. The second time I got a call from his dad saying he had been arrested was my breaking point. He was arrested for driving without insurance and on a suspended license. While this was not a major crime, it still was on his record. Unfortunately, the process is the same regardless of what you get picked up for. This time, I refused his phone calls since I had no intention of posting bail; been there, done that. I didn't sleep that night, I just prayed for God to protect him and give me the wisdom to know what to say to help turn him around. He was a good kid.

Within a couple of months I received a call from his dad that my son needed to stay with me while they were on vacation; he couldn't be trusted to stay alone at their house. Of course, I was glad to get him back, but the rules still applied under my roof. When I knew he was on his way, I prayed to God for the right words to show him that I loved him but still needed him to be mindful of our rules. My husband was not looking forward to him coming home, if even for a week, he didn't trust him. When he got there, we sat down and discussed what my expectations were for the week. I also let him know that he did not have to leave at the end of the week. I would help him get his finances in order so that he could eventually get an apartment or, better still, buy a house; emphasizing the fact that the rules were the same as when he left.

The following Mother's Day he gave me a card and wrote an expression of his appreciation for what I had done for him and the last sentence was "So thank you for being the best mom and friend that anyone could ask for." I thanked God for where He had brought us from and to, and what He had done for our relationship. I continue to pray for him and remind him to always remember that God has brought him to where he is now, and will continue to guide his steps when he turns to Him.

Sandy

About 6 years ago, when I was still married, my husband and I were going through serious financial troubles and were barely making ends meet each month. Actually, most months we were not even doing that. I had three small children then, and my daughter was 6 or 7 at the time when she lost a tooth and was hoping for five dollars from the tooth fairy. The problem was I didn't have five dollars. Not at home, and not in the bank. While she was so excited, I was feeling so defeated. I checked everywhere for money throughout the house. I even checked the couch for change. My plan was to write an IOU note from the tooth fairy. I went to bed in tears and fell asleep praying. I wasn't asking for much. I just wanted to be able to provide for my family. In the middle of the night, I was awoken with the thought so great to 'check Vince's desk'. I told myself I already checked there, but the feeling was so strong it wouldn't escape me. So I got up and went downstairs to look on my husband's desk. There, right in the middle of the desk, laid a brand new, crisp five dollar bill. It took my breath away and I broke into tears. It was a sign to me from God that everything would be ok and he would provide for us and our needs. I will never doubt that, and I will never forget my sign from God and that five dollar bill!

Renee

I had been sick for several weeks suffering with my COPD which ultimately landed me in the emergency room. Thank God I didn't have pneumonia or any infection in my lungs. I'm sure he healed me before I got there! The doctors checked me out and stabilized me before they sent me home with some new medications. My husband and I were struggling financially and didn't have medical or prescription insurance. We had to pay out of pocket, and the thought of paying for the hospital visit was more than we could handle. With that being said, the next day we were trying to figure out how we would be able to afford a new nebulizer, possibly oxygen, and yet another doctor visit. We were getting frustrated and depressed trying to hash it all out. I told my husband, "Let's just quit worrying about it. We will do what we can and pray." He then left to go to the store and I started praying and asking for the Lord's help. It wasn't even thirty minutes later when I heard a knock on my door. When I opened the door, the postman was there with a package from a friend of mine who had no idea what was going on. In the package, was the inhaler that I needed. They didn't need it, and thought of me, and hoped that I could possibly use it. God instantly answered my prayer, and what is even more awesome is that it was answered before I even asked. The mail takes at least two days, so He obviously sent it before I even knew I needed it! Even when we can't figure things out, He has a plan!

Linda

When I met my husband, we liked to go out and party with our friends. I was a 'social drinker' with a limit of 2 drinks since I was always the designated driver. My husband was a heavier drinker, but I had no idea how heavy. I had no idea he was consuming a 5th each day and, even worse, he was doing drugs. I've never been around a functioning addict, so I was blind to what was going on. In fact, I didn't know until years later. A few years after we met, he started having abdominal pains that just wouldn't stop. We went to the doctor several times with no relief. In fact, the PA at the doctor's office told him that the x-ray showed that he was constipated and sent him home with a prescription laxative. The following night he was doubled over in pain, so off to the hospital we went. They took x-rays and an ultrasound and admitted him with a diagnosis of a small blockage in his colon. He was taken off of all solids as we waited for them to schedule surgery to take the blockage out and sew up the colon; not a big deal, right? Wrong. The next day, the 90-minute surgery turned into 5½ hours, and the problem was actually a grapefruit sized mass on his colon that was attaching itself to his bladder. They would be testing the mass for cancer. If nothing else sends you to your knees; that certainly will.

The next morning, my poor husband woke up to find out that he was being tested for cancer and he had a colostomy bag for at least 60 days. By the time I got to the hospital, he was in full blown panic mode and I was too sick to stay with him that day. When I got to the hospital the next day, he told me that he was scared and that during the night, he had called out to God to help him and not let this mass be cancer. The doctor came in later that day and told us that it was not cancer and that at the end of the 60 days they would remove the bag. God not only healed my husband that day, but He also laid it on his heart to stop the drinking and the drugs. He walked away from both and even became part of a group to help recovering addicts at the church. His testimony helped other addicts know that recovery is possible with God's help. We both gave thanks to God for the healing of not only his body, but his addiction.

15

It Just Has to Be!

When something happens where you know beyond a reasonable doubt that it was an intervention from God, because only God could make it happen—it simply takes your breath away and removes all of your fears and doubts. Then there are those times when you sense a loved one is near or something happens that leads you to believe that only God could be behind the occurrence. What other explanation is there? We may try to reason it away, but we can't dismiss the feeling we have deep inside. The warm feeling of love, peace, faith, and belief knowing that He is always with us and, when we need Him the most, He sends us signs that only we can recognize. In the end, it is God who gets us through.

Arlene Garrett

I'm really not sure what it was that I experienced in the middle of the night, but it was something I will never forget. Eighteen years ago, in my second marriage, I lost the love of my life and became a widow. I love and miss this man so much it still hurts. My life has never been the same since his passing. I did, however, remarry and had just recently gone through a horrific divorce.

On this particular evening, I was feeling very sad, depressed, and lonely before falling asleep. Thoughts of my past seemed to dominate my mind and feelings. Falling asleep did not come easy that night. I suppose I was feeling sorry for myself because, ever since I was a little girl, I always wanted to be happily married, and now my life was falling apart once again!

I fell asleep and woke in the middle of the night. As I started to lift my body to get out of bed, I felt a slight pressure on my left shoulder. It really frightened and startled me. I quickly looked to my left, saw nothing, and lay back down. I wondered what had just happened. After a few seconds, I started to raise my body to get up again. Only this time, the pressure on my left shoulder was a bit more forceful. I immediately lay down again, and when I did the most wonderful feeling of peace began to come over me. What happened in those following moments, or however long it was, can only be described as a spiritual encounter of some kind. There is just no other explanation for what I experienced that night.

It felt as if I was magically brought back in time and into the arms of the love of my life once again. As I said earlier, it had been 18 years since his passing, but he looked like he did when we first met and fell in love. I seemed to be in a gazebo type of setting. He slowly walked toward me and reached out his hand to me. He then sat down next to me and we talked for what seemed to be a very long time. Then he held me in his arms and kissed me with such love and passion that I didn't want it to end. I had longed for his touch and his arms around me for so long, and on this night his embrace was the most comforting feeling I had ever experienced. It was so real and wonderful! Before he faded out of my life in this dream, or whatever this experience was, he hugged me so tight I could hardly breathe. He then simply said, *"Don't be scared. I'm right here. Always have been, and always will."* He then pulled me to a standing position and hugged me one last time. Slowly, he began to walk backwards. I started getting upset as he very slowly; as if in slow motion, turned his back, then slightly turned to reach his arm back out to me and continued to walk away. I remember very vividly as he was fading out of my life, that he seemed to be surrounded by what seemed to be like a fog. I started shouting, *"No! Don't go! Come back!"* and didn't stop until he was gone.

After this experience, when I was fully awake, I simply could not believe what had just happened. I can't say it was a dream, because truly it was not. I remember asking God, *"What was that, Lord? What just happened?"* I didn't feel that I could share this with anyone, for fear of them not believing me. I decided to go to the store to just walk around. I wasn't going there for anything in particular; I just couldn't get the events of the night before out of my mind. I aimlessly went up and down a few aisles, when I seemed to be directed to the card section of the store. I was led directly to a specific spiritual card that immediately drew my attention. I picked this card up and when I started to read the message, it was like God was talking directly to me. I was in awe. I read the words, *"God doesn't wait for us to reach out, to ask for help, and get on our knees. God just goes ahead and takes our hands before we ask."* When I opened the card to read the inside message, I was brought to tears right there where I stood. The words in this card happened to be the exact words that my deceased husband said to me the night before. I could not believe my eyes when I read, *"Don't be scared. I'm right here. Always have been, always will."* In tears, the reality set in. Even now it gives me chills, as I reminisce about the events of that night.

Thank you, God, for letting me know how real that night's experience was! You are an "awesome" God. This card is now neatly tucked away in my Bible. I take it out every so often, and reflect on that special night God gave us together, if only for a short while.

Diana

My family and my best friend's family go on vacation together to Ocean City every year. On this particular day we were at the beach, and we stayed really late. The beach was almost totally cleared of people. We were gathering the kids together as they were busy playing in the sand. When I looked over, they were forming a cross in the sand. At that point, this warm feeling and the sense of the Lord came over me and I knew He was with us. The sun was beaming and it was such a beautiful feeling. We finally gathered everyone together and we were walking on the wood ramp to get to the boardwalk. My friend's oldest son stopped and said there was something red peeking through the sand. It was a tiny red rubbery cross that just showed up out of nowhere. As we were walking back to the condo, on the same street in front of where we were staying, there was a car that had a picture of a cross in its back window. That car stayed there for approximately three more days in the same spot! I will never forget that whole experience!! I know in my heart that the only hands in that experience belonged to the Lord!!!

Cheryl

When I was moving some items to our new house, I had a Grandfathers clock that was made for me by my Great-Grandfather that had not worked for years and years. I was stopped at a red light at an intersection, and when it turned green, the clock started the bonging noise it would make on the hour. I was surprised by it, and hit the brakes because I couldn't believe what I was hearing. As I did that, there was a car accident in front of me where two cars collided head on. Had it not been for the bong of my Great-Grandfather's clock, I would have been sandwiched between those two cars if I had not stopped in awe. The clock is still with me and has never made a sound. My grandfathers were both looking out for me.

Michele

My son was in a horrible motorcycle accident last May. He snapped his leg in half with bones sticking out from his skin; he had deep to-the-bone lacerations on both of his feet, horrible road rash, and minor cuts and bruises. It was 3am and after sliding across the asphalt about 30-feet, he came to a stop. He saw something shining in the road and crawled 50-feet to see what it was. The accident took place on a dark country road, and believe it or not, his cell phone flash light was on. If you know about iPhones, you know you need to push a button to get it to come on. The thing that makes this story so amazing is that my father, his grandfather, had just passed away that November, six months before his accident. We believe that he was there and turned the light on for my son so he could call for help! To this day, I thank whomever it was that helped him get the medical attention he needed that night! My son is now walking on his own without assistance. He still has many scars from that horrible night, but I'm proud to say he's alive and well!

Cheryl

My grandfather and I were so very, very, close. He committed suicide when I was in fourth grade. He had melanoma and there was no cure at that time. After visiting us, and knowing how sick he was, he took his life. The morning this happened, my mom gave me the phone as he had called to talk to me, like always. We talked about special moments and things we had done together. We talked about going to the farms that he was very involved with in 4H and how the farmers loved him. My grandmother called not long after, to say he had died early that morning. I remember my mom saying, "No . . . he had just called and had just spoken to me." She kept repeating, "No, no, he just called." My mom, dad, and I were shocked and didn't believe my grandmother. I had spoken to him when he was already gone. How could that be?

Rene

Three months after my husband passed away things were very hard for me. The kids and I were now living in a new state, a new home, and I was trying to keep the kids together by myself in a town where we knew no one. One day we were out in the car running errands and I stopped at an intersection. So much was going through my mind, and I was missing my husband terribly. At that moment, when all of my thoughts were on him, I felt a kiss on my cheek and the scent of him was overwhelming. My initial reaction was my daughter must have seen a tear on my cheek, and kissed me. I yelled at her to stay in her seat and not lean over to kiss me. When I looked back at her, not only was she still in her seat with the seatbelt on, but I had made her cry because I had yelled at her. This is when I realized it had to have been my husband who kissed me; letting me know it was going to be alright. The tears rolled out of my eyes as I apologized to my daughter, and I sighed with relief knowing he was with us watching over us and that everything was going to be okay!

Jean

One night driving down Fannie Dorsey Road, something told me to stop. It was just a voice in my head, an intuition of sorts, or was it God? I decided to listen to that voice and I actually stopped right in the middle of the road. At that split second when my car came to a halt, I was amazed to see several deer come darting out from behind a bush in the open field and they ran right out into the road in front of me. I sat there in total disbelief. Had I not stopped when I did, I certainly would have hit at least one of those deer. I know it was God who put the thought in my head to stop.

Michelle

Two days after my dad passed away I was in the car driving by myself. I missed him so much and was having such a hard time dealing with his death. In the past, he was usually always with me since I took him to various doctor's appointments and ran all of his errands. With a heavy heart, I was alone in the car driving, when, out of nowhere, I smelled his cologne. The scent was so strong, as if he just put it on. Then just as suddenly as it appeared, it disappeared ten minutes later. It was January, but not cold enough for the heat to be on and the windows were up. I believe it was God's way of helping me realize that even though I can no longer see my dad, he is always with me!

Sharon

I have owned several dogs and I loved them all dearly. Conan was a big, gentle Pit Bull. He was beautiful, and loving, but he also loved to get in the trash can. No matter what I did, he would find a way. After he passed, we were sitting in the kitchen one day, when, out of nowhere, the lid just popped off the trash can and fell to the floor. There was nothing near the trashcan that we could see. Dumbstruck, we just looked at each other with a grin and said, "Conan!"

Stacie

One day, I was at the Zoo in Hershey Park where they had a field filled with huge bucks. I told my mom that was the first time I EVER saw a live buck in person. I have, however, seen a million doe's. Then one night driving back home from work on an old windy road, where it is pretty common for deer to run out on the road, my mind was on auto-pilot. This was not unusual since I drive this road almost every day. When all of the sudden, that conversation I had with my mom at the Zoo started replaying in my head and I kept picturing a huge buck. It was long after that when, for some reason, I grabbed the steering wheel with both hands. Right then, a HUGE buck literally jumped off the hill into the road directly in front of me! I was so startled, that I just sat there for a minute. Apparently, the person coming the other way on the road was freaked out too, because they just sat there for a minute as well. Then another smaller deer jumped down too. If I hadn't replayed that conversation with my mom in my head, and hadn't grabbed the wheel with both hands being very cautious at that exact moment, I think it could have been much worse. God decided to take the wheel that night!

Cindy

As my great-aunt lay on her deathbed, she said to me, "You are stronger than you realize, and you're going to realize just how strong you are." I told my sisters later that it kind of freaked me out. This happened in January of 2010. It was in April, 2010, when my husband was diagnosed with ALS. He passed away in October of 2012, quickly followed by his mom, and then my dad. As if that wasn't enough, six weeks after my dad, I lost my mom! That's a lot of loss in a 14-month span of time for anyone to handle. My husband's two and half year battle with ALS, was the toughest. I had to be strong for him and our twins, who were 12 when he passed. My aunt was right. I am stronger than I realized! Somehow she 'knew' what was coming and what I was going to have to deal with, and I am thankful for her words of encouragement as they continually pull me through tough times!

Danii

I'm a recovering addict and the day I surrendered to God, I was at my rock bottom. I found myself lying on the ground praying. While I lay there crying and praying, I asked God to be my rock. Shortly after, I began to regain my composure. As I attempted to get back up, I moved my hand under me on the ground to support my weight. It was then that I felt something hard under my hand, and all my focus went immediately to what was causing me pain. When I looked down, it was a perfectly round rock! I remember thinking to myself, 'Wow! That is weird!' I took that as my sign from God and I've been clean ever since. I still have the rock. When times get tough I go back to the rock and God, and know that He has my back and He is my Rock!

Erin

I was born and raised Catholic and I was raised by my Mother, as a single parent, as my parents divorced when I was only a toddler. I would only see my dad one or two days of the week, mostly only a few hours at a time. Years later, I was about to go through my Confirmation at church. Friday was the rehearsal, and then a dance for the students was after rehearsal. I originally invited my parents to come, but decided last minute that it was not necessary, and that we could see one another Sunday morning. Dad stopped by Friday night after work just to say, 'hello' and I told him to get to church early; knowing he liked to sleep in. I told him I loved him, gave him a kiss and we parted ways.

When Sunday morning came, I had both friends and family in the church and I was eager to have another sacrament behind me. Before mass begun, I got the worst feeling rush over me. I looked up at the crucifix and had a huge lump in my throat. My heart started beating out of control. My hands were sweaty. I took a look back at my relatives and my dad was nowhere in sight. Something awful has happened. I just knew it.

The celebration went on, and a party followed at the house afterward. I still didn't feel right. It was odd. All I kept hearing was my mother saying stupid things about my dad not being there. That was typical of her . . . putting him down. I didn't want to hear it, so I found a quiet place to myself where I could be alone. It's hard to explain, but a feeling of emptiness came over me. I knew he was dead. It's as if I could no longer feel him "present". After many phone calls and voice mails left at his apartment, he had been found in his bedroom by my uncle. The deterioration of his body clearly indicated that he had been gone for about a week. Phone calls were made and apparently our house was the last to receive the news. Seven days later, my mom crept up the stairs and knocked on my bedroom door. Her face was pained. She looked as if she had aged overnight. It was the week before finals during my sophomore year in high school when I got the worse news of my life, but like I said . . . I already knew.

It was because of God that I knew of my father's passing before my mother even told me, nearly a week later. Call it intuition; call it miraculous; or call it what you want, but I knew because God gave me the information I needed to help me come to terms with his death!

Debbie

My husband and I were in Hawaii on vacation celebrating his 50th birthday and excited for sight-seeing and diving excursions. Dave was in perfect health, so we thought. Yeah, he was twenty pounds overweight, yet all of his blood work and blood pressure were great. Blood pressure always ran around 120/80 with no blips on the radar. Dave was often described by many friends as someone bigger than life, super strong and had a huge heart! Little did we know, his heart was actually two times larger than average. In the end, doctors couldn't believe there were no other signs and we had no idea. His condition had been like this for years, unbeknownst to us or his family doctor.

It was ten days into our trip, when he said his chest felt funny. Despite my concern and desire to have him checked out at the local hospital, he brushed it off to having eaten a greasy meal at dinner and being in the sun all day. He argued the point, saying, "I'm fine. I'm sure I would know if I was having a heart attack." The next day, he again said he was fine and he seemed to be perfectly normal to me. As I look back now, in hind-sight, he did seem to be a bit confused at times during the dive. He had expressed some feelings of anxiety, but again, he brushed that off to the possibility of seeing a Tiger Shark during our upcoming dive later that morning. I tried to talk with him again about how he was feeling, but he responded frustrated and annoyed, positive that it was anxiety as it only happened when he thought about seeing the shark. Again, despite my concerns, we pushed forward with our diving trip.

During the dive, I turned around to look for Dave and didn't see him. We were supposed to be heading back to the shore line because he was already running out of air. Frantically, I'm looking everywhere for him until I finally spot him on the shoreline starting to take off his gear. Instantly, I'm frustrated because he just 'left' me out in the Ocean by myself; which is very unlike Dave. When he recognized my frustrations, he immediately started apologizing. I remember the look on his face. His eyes were so very sad and he was obviously very sorry. We started to head back to our truck and he appeared fine, other than being apologetic. He navigated over uneven lava rocks and had the wherewithal to let me know when I started to go the wrong way. When we got back to the truck, which was maybe ¼ mile away from where we entered the water, he started to explain, "You don't understand, I just didn't feel right." At that moment, I didn't care what he said, we were going to the hospital whether he liked it, or not. He began arguing vehemently against the idea, and even going so far as to say that he wasn't going. He raised his voice, "They can't treat me without my permission." I rolled my eyes, shook my head, and walked around to the other side of the truck to start changing out of my gear when I heard him make an awful sound. I immediately ran back around to find Dave gasping for breath, face already purple, and staggering as though he was about to fall. We were about a half-mile away from anything populated, and no other cars or people anywhere in sight. Still I screamed out for help, desperate and scared, and yelled to him I was going to call 911 as I ran back around the truck to get my phone. I had no idea what was going on – was it a heart attack? Did he touch something while diving that could be causing an allergic reaction? Was he choking? Nothing made sense. Out of nowhere, a diver appeared and asked if everything was okay. I had no idea where he came from, but I said "I think my husband is having heart attack." This stranger went right over and started giving him CPR. It was like he just appeared. He was very calm, patient, and just handled the situation. He worked on him for thirteen minutes until the EMT's arrived. Later, I found out this stranger just so happened to be a doctor. When the EMT's arrived, they had to shock him to bring him back. He responded and became alert, but in obvious pain. Unsure of whether this episode was a result of the dive with his oxygen, altitude issues, or heart related, they couldn't give him any medication until they could rule things out. Once in the hospital, they had to shock him again. This time though, they couldn't get him stabilized. They had been working on him for about 45 minutes at the hospital. I was standing in the background out of their way as I watched them work on him. I saw all the instrument panels flat line. Then, as if in slow motion, they began stepping away from

Dave as if they were giving up. The doctors checked again for a pulse and documented his time of death. I was numb. The doctor came over to me and said "I'm sorry, there's nothing more we can do." I told the doctor not to stop – to keep trying, that he wasn't gone. The doctor put his hand on my shoulder and simply said, "I'm sorry for your loss." I looked at the Chaplain shaking my head, wanting for someone to understand and to help me. She too said she was sorry. I immediately ran over to Dave. Somehow, I knew he wasn't gone. I leaned down to kiss his cheek, and as soon as my lips touched his skin, I felt his breath on my cheek and heard two shallow puffs of very faint air. I knew immediately that he was still here, he was trying desperately to breathe. I knew it was not his last breathes for air. He was still with us! I yelled over to the nurse who was turning off all the equipment, but he just shook his head no and said "it's not that". But I knew it was. I turned to the chaplain again and saw the amazed look on her face as she said, "I see what you're seeing." I then screamed out for someone to come help my husband. The nurse reappeared, and I saw the look of annoyance turn instantly to shock as he reached down to feel for a pulse. The doctor appeared just then and the nurse stated, as though in disbelief, "He's breathing and . . . he has a pulse?" The doctor immediately replied, "Hook him up!" I smiled and said, "I told you . . . you just don't know my husband. He's too strong and too stubborn to go that easily!" For five hours I sat with him as he lay in that bed breathing on his own with no help or assistance. He was determined to hold on to what life he had with the strength he had left.

The doctors decided since he had been stable for that period of time, they would put him on a plane and transport him to another Hawaiian Island, Oahu, where they had a cardiac center better equipped to handle his condition. While on the plane and getting ready to begin the initial descent in preparation of landing, you know that sinking feeling in your stomach when that occurs, it was at that exact moment when I saw a tear drop down from his right eye. I wiped it away, but this time I knew that that was him telling me he had to go. They immediately began working on him through the descent and the whole way to the hospital. At the hospital they continued to work on him as they couldn't seem to stabilize him. Finally, the cardiac surgeon came over to me and stated, "His heart is still beating, but we can't get a pulse. Do you know what that means?" And I did. His brain was getting no oxygen. That Dave, as I knew him, was gone.

God had given me those extra hours with Dave, to come to terms with the loss I would suffer and to give me the time I needed for some closure. It would be just like Dave to say, "God, just give me a minute and I'll be right back!" Only God, can create a miracle like that. Only He can bring someone back to life, even if only for a few hours. Thank God for giving us that time together!

Later that week, I was back on a plane heading home with Dave's ashes in my arms. What happened next was something that is so hard to explain, and people may think I'm crazy, but I know I was not asleep and that there is something so much larger than life, that it can only be God. Probably, only those of you that have experienced something similar will understand. I was sitting on the plane, with my head back and eyes closed but clearly awake. It was at that exact moment when the plane starts to descent preparing for landing, yes that same moment I saw the tear fall from Dave's eye just days before, when I felt someone take my hand and lift my arm. Though I knew my arm was still on the arm rest, it was as if the hand being lifted was my spirit's hand - almost as if I had two of the same. What I began seeing is indescribable. The best way to describe it would a sense of being surrounded by white, wispy clouds and colors in motion everywhere. Such vibrant colors in shapes of ovals, not like streaks of colors or rays at all. At the time, I didn't know what the colors were, only that they were beautiful and mesmerizing. I later wondered if they could have been entities of colorful souls. I was moving forward through the clouds, yet felt no breeze, no sound, and had no words. I have no idea how long it lasted as I had no sense of time. I would guess it couldn't have been longer than a minute or two based on where we were in the descent from when it started to when it ended. However, while I didn't have a sense of time, I did, have such a sense of peace within my very soul. As I was moving forward through the clouds, I saw a light and dark figure of a man far off in the distance, but getting closer. I was mesmerized by it. Then, just like that, it was over. The feeling, the images – it all disappeared. I kept opening and closing my eyes trying to recapture the feeling, the images, and wondering, what was that? Take me back! I know I was awake, yet I know I just experienced something so miraculous that only God can explain. In my heart, I believe that it was Dave showing me that he was okay. Dave always took care of me, and he always had to "show me". He was never one that was happy with just talking or describing; he always had to take it to the next level, and show you.

16

In Closing

For all the signs we receive, whether they are from God, loved ones that have passed away, or even our beloved pets, they will forever share a special place in our hearts and fill us with peace and joy when we are open enough to recognize them. These signs give us comfort in knowing there is a powerful force much greater than you and I. As our faith and spirituality continues to grow, we become more receptive to messages from God, bringing us closer to Him. God speaks to us in many ways. It may be an inner voice you hear in your head, a dream you have, angels sent to you, or it might be an extraordinary spiritual encounter. No matter how He speaks to you, take the time to listen, and follow His lead. He knows the right path for you, and will continue to lead you to your destiny.

Ever since I was a child, I wanted to write a book. I remember hiding from my brother in my closet where I would spend hours writing by the light of my Lite-Brite. Throughout the years I dabbled in it; but it was

God this time that pushed me to actually step out of my comfort zone, and practically demanded, *"Just do it!"* This journey has truly been driven by God himself. He has led me every step of the way to where I needed to be, and has given me the courage to just do it. He provides us with signs from Heaven in a way that only He can do.

God created every one of us to be successful. He has a plan in place and if we follow, He will lead us to where we need to be, in His time. He will put people and circumstances in our lives that will make us stronger. These circumstances, miraculous moments, and signs that cross our path are not ordinary. They are destiny-altering, and they can and will change our lives forever. Even though you may not see a lot of what you consider good breaks right now, be encouraged because His plan will thrust you forward with blessings of favor. We encourage you to look for the signs and follow His lead. All things are possible through God!

ABOUT THE AUTHORS

Sharon Shabinaw & Arlene Garrett

A mother and daughter's dream coming true . . .
We would always correct each other, saying, "*You* are
the wind beneath *my* wings." "NO! *You* are the wind
beneath *my* wings." We have both now come to realize
that it is truly God who is the wind beneath *our* wings
in so many ways. Our writing journey has been a
work-in-progress for 35 years and now, through a
chain of events and intervention from God, we are
finally ready to spread the word so that you, our
readers, can benefit knowing that miracles do happen if
you never give up hope and truly believe.

Signs from God is our first book together. It
depicts the intervention from God who clearly is
working through us and leading us every step of the
way on this journey. We've shared ways in which God
has touched our lives so profoundly. At times it just
takes our breath away as we sit back in awe, in the
comfort of His arms, knowing He is in control. *Signs
from God* is a compilation of stories relating how God
has touched our lives as well as many others we have
connected with in our community. Arlene shares her
testimony as she describes in great detail the miracle
that she experienced after suffering with a nervous
breakdown for five years. Each story is amazing in its
own way and will leave you feeling uplifted and in

touch with your own "Signs from God" and learning to recognize how He communicates with all of us.

Follow us on our continued journey of documenting even more signs from God of prayers answered, and also unanswered. Even though your prayers may not have been answered at the time, it's those unanswered prayers perhaps that really helped you recognize God's plan for you. We believe there are a lot of these stories out there—won't you share in the joy of spreading God's message for others to be hopeful, uplifted, and know that God is working in their lives even when we can't see it at the time? It is our hope and prayer that this book has done just that for you.

Connect and share your stories with us through
www.facebook.com/groups/SignsfromGod

You can also follow us through our blog
www.windbeneathourwings1980.blogspot.com

WHAT'S NEXT . . .

We truly believe this book, and all of the signs from God that we have received, is paving the way for our ultimate journey and many books to come. After 35 years, we are now in the process of putting pen to paper reliving the miracle that took place in our lives in the year 1980. It has been our goal to publish our story, *A Mountain to Climb*, which depicts and elaborates in detail the pain and torment of suffering through a nervous breakdown, the events that led up to it, and the effect it had not only on the patient but the family as well. As you read the breathtaking experience of the miraculous healing that took place after first turning her back on God and then being given the breath of life from God, you will not be able to put the book down! It's written from Arlene's perspective, as the patient suffering for nearly five years of her nightmare, as well as flashbacks from her daughter, Sharon's eyes at a vulnerable time in her life, and witnessing this at a time when she needed her mother the most.

Made in the USA
San Bernardino, CA
21 October 2015